Non-Fiction Titles by Janvier T. Chando
UNBROKEN III: THE HOLY LAND—The Roman and Byzantine Empires…
HEGEMON IN THE MAKING: THE BIRTH AND GROWTH…
FALLEN HEROES: African Leaders Whose Assassinations…
ICONS AND VILLAINS: Recent Political Assassinations…
UKRAINE: The Tug-of-War Between Russia and the West
CAMEROON: The Haunted Heart of Africa

Fiction Titles by Janvier Chando

The Usurper: and Other Stories
Triple Agent, Double Cross
Disciples of Fortune
The Union Moujik
Flash of the Sun
Fortune Calls
Fortune's Master
The Girl on the Trail
Fortune's Children
The Norilsk Bears
Me Before Them
The Fire and Ice Legend
The Sweetest Madness
The Grandmothers
The Hunger Fire
The Shades of Fire
Father and Sons
Fateful Ties
The Verdict of Hades
His Majesty's Trial
Ngoko's Folly
The Usurper
The Dowry
I am Hated
The Oaf

Upcoming Titles by Janvier Chando

The Home Drifters
The Mortal Friends
The White Hawk
Splendid Comets

FALLEN HEROES:
African Leaders Whose Assassinations Disarrayed the Continent and Benefitted Foreign Interests

Janvier T. Chando

TISI BOOKS

NEW YORK, RALEIGH, LONDON, AMSTERDAM

PUBLISHED BY TISI BOOKS
www.tisibooks.com

FALLEN HEROES:
African Leaders Whose Assassinations Disarrayed the Continent and Benefitted Foreign Interests

ISBN-13: 978-1-9809-9669-9
ISBN-10: 1-9809-9669-5

PUBLISHED BY TISI BOOKS
www.tisibooks.com

NEW YORK, RALEIGH, LONDON, AMSTERDAM

Printed in The United States of America

EPIGRAPH

"Destiny is something we can only contemplate, but fate, we can influence."
—*CHRISTOPHER NKWAYEP-CHANDO*

Acknowledgement

My deepest, warmest and everlasting thanks to Dr. Samuel F. Tchwenko and Christopher N. Chando for their contributions to the ideal of social solidarity and the enhancement of humanity.

DEDICATION

The book is dedicated to all of Africa's iconic and legendary leaders whose purposes were to serve their people and humanity, and to advance the wellbeing of mankind, especially those African leaders who were cut short in their historic missions by the evil forces of this world.

FALLEN HEROES:
African Leaders Whose Assassinations Disarrayed the Continent and Benefitted Foreign Interests

Contents

Maps

Political Map of Africa

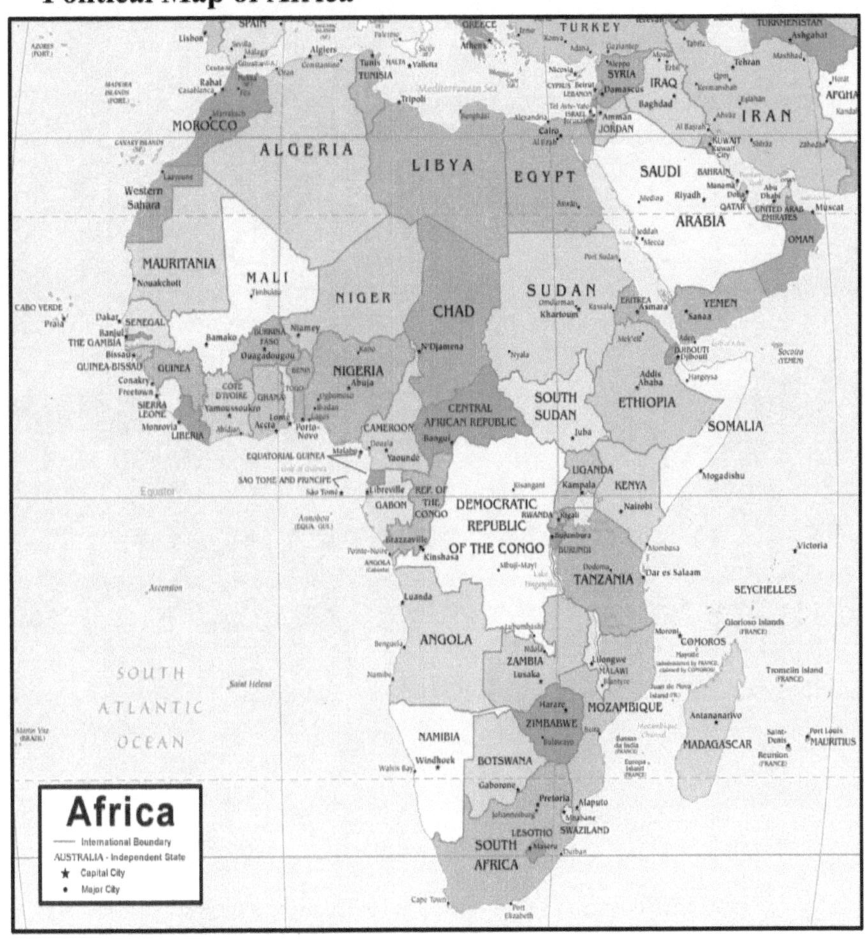

Africa before the 1884 Berlin Conference that partitioned it

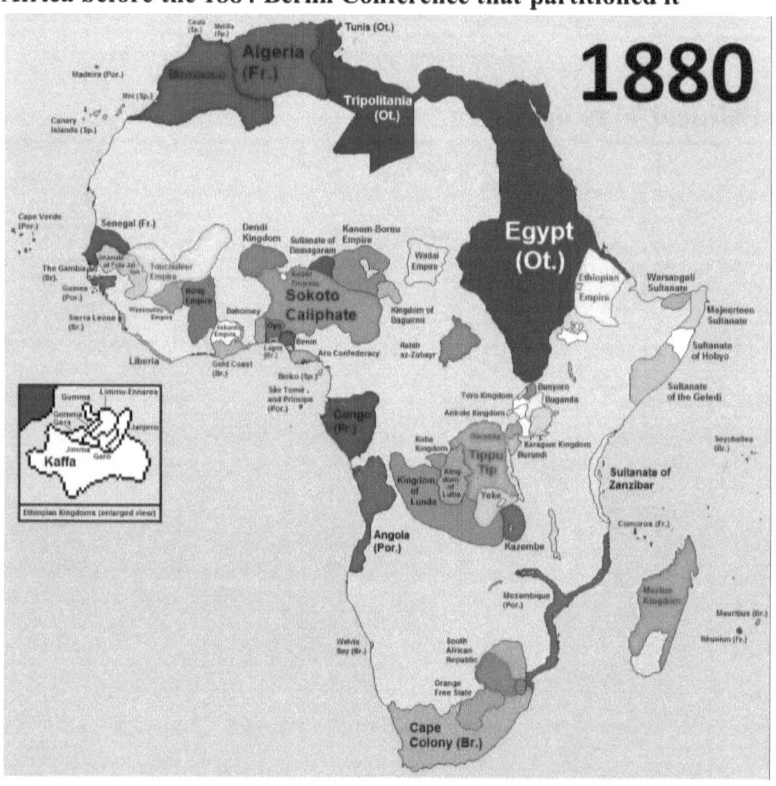

Partition Map of Africa: 1884-1914

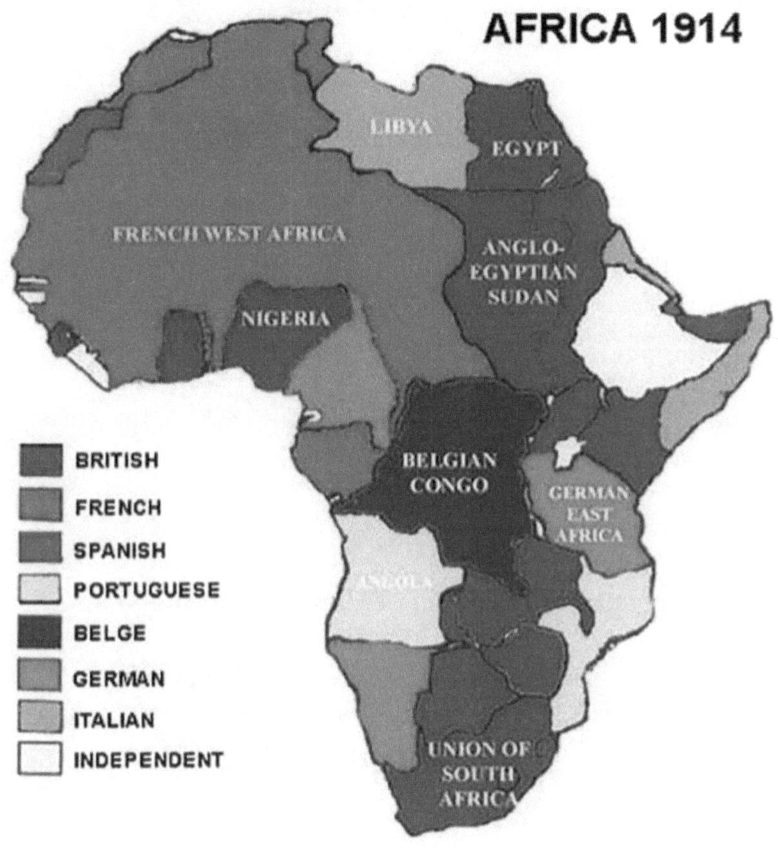

Africa Independence Dates --- Decolonization of Africa

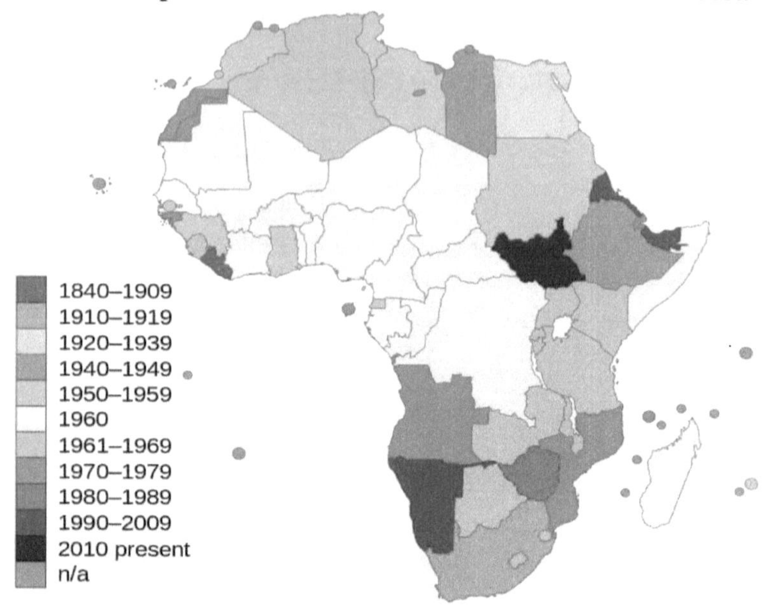

The Measure of Freedom of Countries of the World

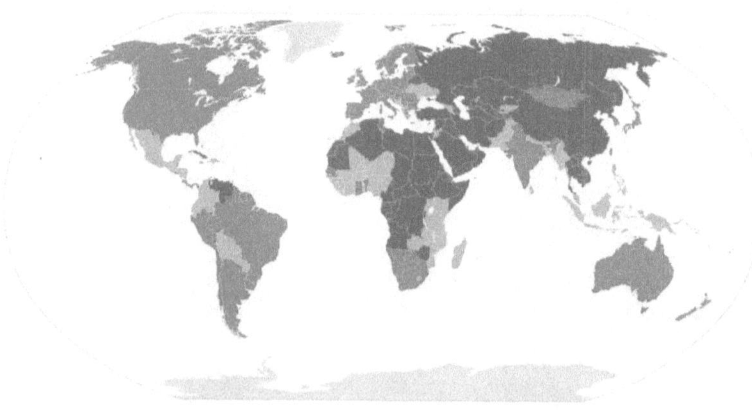

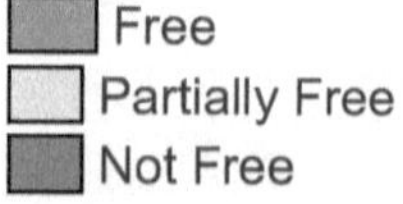

2016 Democracy Rating of African Countries

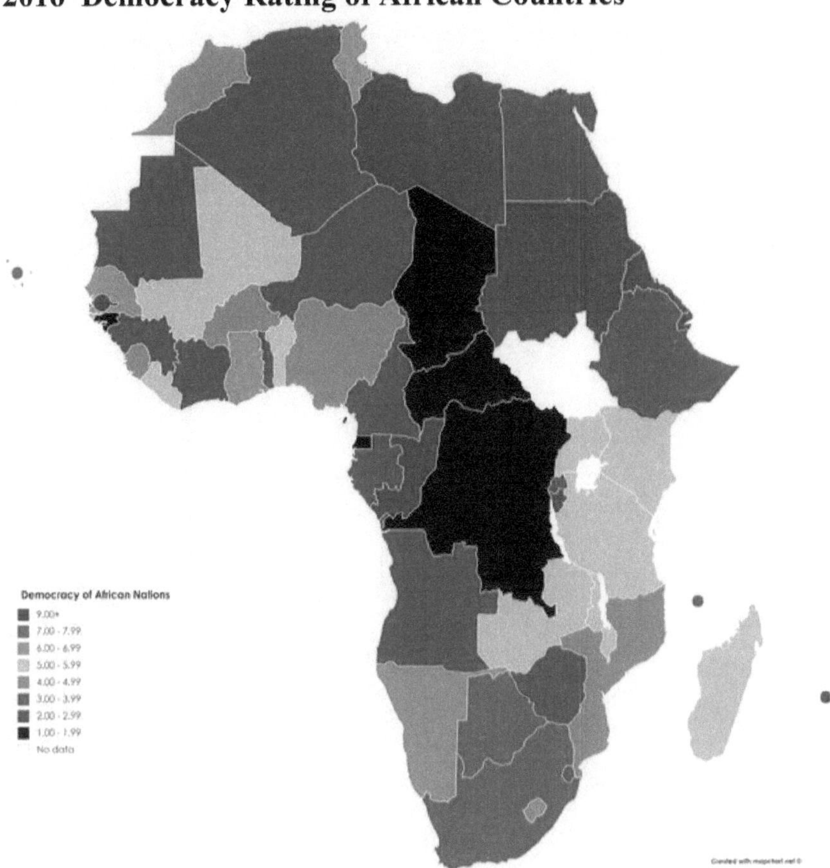

The use of political assassinations against key leaders of liberation movements has had a major impact on the course of history in Africa and the Middle East. Not only have some of the greatest of Third World leaders been killed, but so, too, has the hope for political change they embodied.

- Victoria Brittain

PROLEGOMENON

No continent suffered the horrendous effects of slavery as much as Africa; no continent was ravished by colonialism as much as the land that is the cradle of civilization, and no continent has been exploited and is being exploited like the world's second-largest and second most populous continent. When we take into account the fact that the African continent is more resources-endowed than the others; when the harsh reality hits us that it is the least developed of the world's main continuous expanses of land; and when we observe that it is haunted by an unbelievable disconnect between the ruling elites and the masses, we then find ourselves confronted by many unavoidable questions such as:

- Why is Africa in such a pathetic state?
- Is the continent incapable of coming up with leaders that can take it out of its current impasse and futile consensus to a future that would advance the wellbeing of the African people?
- Are Pan-Africanists (Africans who are selflessly dedicated to the well-being and development of the land and its people) capable of overhauling its few indigenous dictators and the forces controlling the African puppets — political leaderships and political establishments put in place by foreign

powers and foreign interest — and so bring about the long-awaited reality of a "New Africa" that is economically united, politically integrated and that is in control of its sovereignty?

The first paragraph, in a way, answers the first question. The second and third questions are in the affirmative for the obvious reasons. Pan-Africanist leaders dominated Africa's history in the 1950s and 1960s, and many of them were killed by the colonial and former colonial powers or their agents. In fact, six African independence leaders were assassinated by their ex-colonial rulers between 1961 and 1973.

Were it not that it is sadly true, the list of the killed leaders of African independence movements and the stories behind their deaths or assassinations would make an espionage bestseller.

The first major test of killing the leader of an African independence movement began in Cameroon following the return to power of General Charles De Gaulle in France in June 1958. We are talking here about the September 13, 1958, assassination of Ruben Um Nyobè. He was the leader of the "Union of the Populations of the Cameroons" (UPC), a civic-nationalist political party that was advocating for the reunification and independence of French Cameroon and British Cameroons (territories of the former German Kamerun, which was partitioned between France and Britain following the defeat of Germany in the First World War).

Cameroon suffered another traumatizing assassination

two years after Um Nyobè's gruesome political murder. This was the assassination of Ruben Um Nyobè's successor and second leader of the UPC, Dr. Felix Moumie. He died on November 3, 1960, in Geneva, Switzerland, from thallium poisoning that the French secret agent William Bechtel administered during dinner that they were having together at a restaurant in the Swiss city. The Frenchman had won the Cameroonian's trust by posing as a journalist.

Then there would be Patrice Lumumba, the prime minister of the newly independent Congo, the cruelly ravished former Belgian Congo that from 1885-1908 was known as "The Congo Free State" — essentially the private possession of the Belgian King Leopold II, where more than half of the population died from the effects of exploiting the land's resources. Lumumba's death involving four major Western countries and their agents in Congo is the single biggest cause of the chronic malady of that country, which, like Cameroon, is yet to recover from the trauma it suffered during the early years of its so-called independence.

Sylvanus Olympio, the leader of Togo, would be killed in 1963, barely two years after the assassination of Patrice Lumumba.

Sylvanus Olympio's death would be followed shortly after by that of Mehdi Ben Barka, the leader of the Moroccan opposition movement, who was kidnapped in France in 1965, was never released, and whose body has not been found since then.

Eduardo Mondlane, the leader of Mozambique's FRELIMO (*Frente de Libertação de Moçambique*) or

Liberation Front of Mozambique, which was fighting for the colony's independence from Portuguese rule, would die from a parcel bomb in 1969.

The 1973 assassination of Amilcar Cabral, the leader of the African Party for the Independence of Guinea and Cape Verde, (*Partido Africano da Independência da Guiné e Cabo Verde or PAIGC*), the West African liberation movement against Portuguese colonial rule in Guinea Bissau and Cape Verde, would herald the transition to a new phase of neocolonialism dominated by puppet dictators in the continent who would face little or no pushback from the Pan-Africanist, except in the case of Guinea Bissau, Angola, Mozambique, Namibia and South Africa under Portuguese colonial rule, and under the quasi-colonial rule of Apartheid South Africa respectively.

There have been several other traumatizing assassinations of progressive African political figures in the last six decades. However, the ones below have been the most reverberating, with unintended consequences, as the legacies of these felled African heroes are expanding every day to become the basis for the rebirth of Pan-Africanism, the ideal around which the economic union and political integration of Africa would be realized.

Chapter One

Syria is bad enough; it's a pretty terrible atrocity. But there are much worse ones in the world. So, for example, the worst atrocities in the past decade have been in the Congo, the Eastern Congo, where maybe 5 million people have been killed.

Noam Chomsky — October 8, 2013

Patrice Lumumba

Patrice Lumumba Quotes

"The colonialists care nothing for Africa for her own sake. They are attracted by African riches, and their actions are guided by the desire to preserve their interests in Africa against the wishes of the African people. For the colonialists, all means are good if they help them to possess these riches."

"The day will come when history will speak. But it will not be the history that will be taught in Brussels, Paris, Washington, or the United Nations…Africa will write its own history and in both north and south, it will be a history of glory and dignity."

"Political independence has no meaning if it is not accompanied by rapid economic and social development."

"Without dignity, there is no liberty, without justice, there is no dignity, and without independence, there are no free men."

"A minimum of comfort is necessary for the practice of virtue."

"The only thing which we wanted for our country is the right to a worthy life, to dignity without pretense, to independence without restrictions. This was never the desire of the Belgian colonialists and their Western allies…"

"These divisions, which the colonial powers have always exploited to dominate us, have played an important role — and are still playing that role — in the suicide of Africa."

"We know that Africa is neither French, nor British, nor American, nor Russian, that it is African. We know the objects of the West. Yesterday, they divided us on the level of tribe, clan, and village…They want to create antagonistic blocs, satellites…"

"No one is perfect in this imperfect world."

"African unity and solidarity are no longer dreams. They must be expressed in decisions."

"Freeing the spirit of the African people will be a harder struggle than eradicating the settler colonial regimes."

Congo on a Map of the World

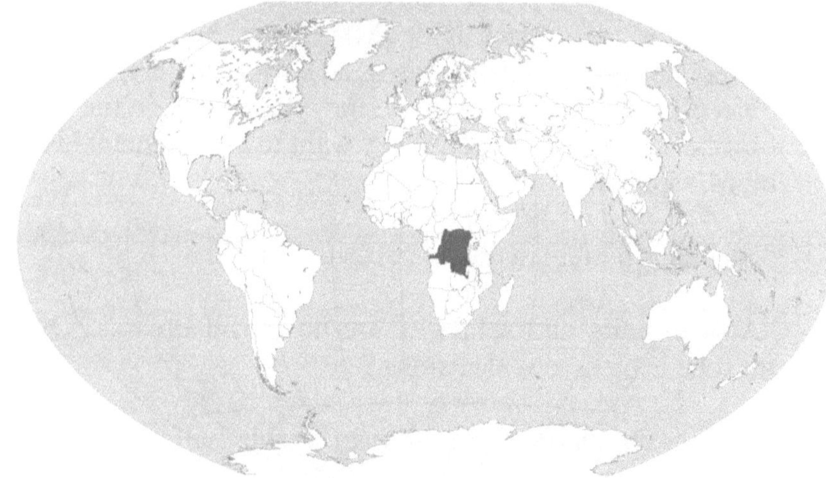

Administrative Map of the Democratic Republic of Congo, 1960

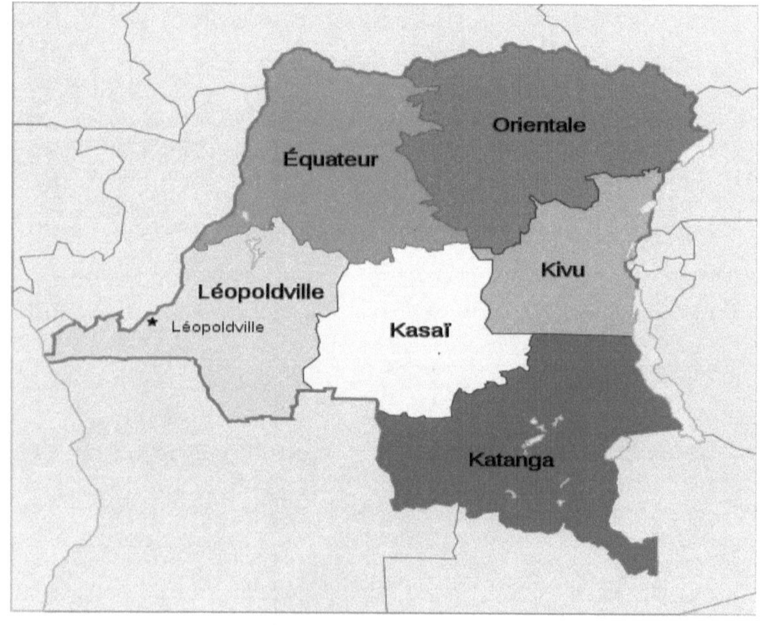

Administrative Map of the Democratic Republic of Congo, 2019

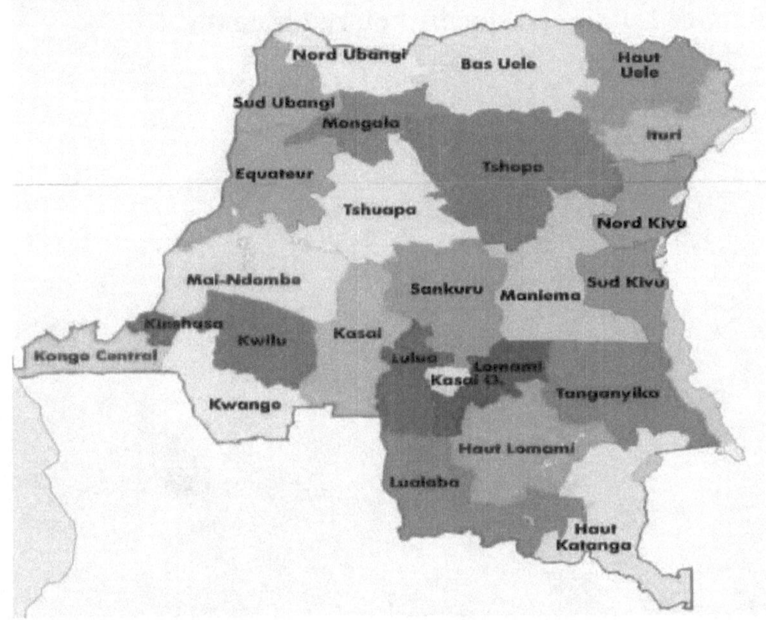

Colonization of Africa and Dates of Independence

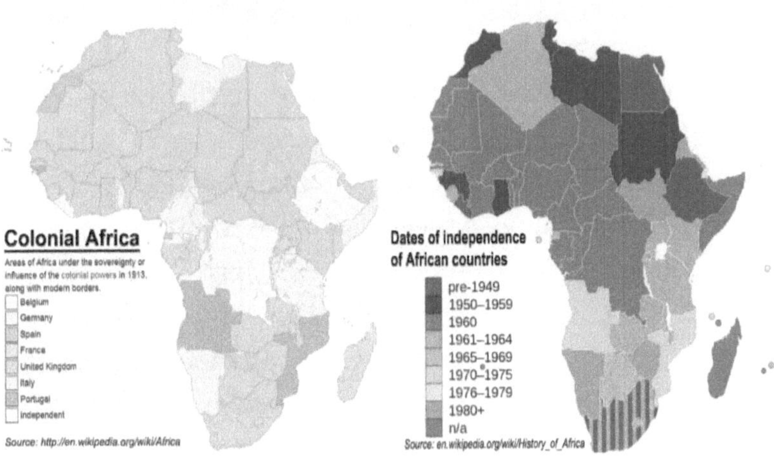

Patrice Lumumba shortly before his death

The January 17, 1961, assassination of Patrice Lumumba, the first democratically elected prime minister of what is today the Democratic Republic of the Congo (DRC), is considered by many Africans as "the most important assassination of the 20th century" because it not only wrecked the country, but it also polarized and paralyzed Africa, resulting in disunity that the continent has yet to recover from. This heinous crime was a culmination of two inter-related assassination plots by elements within the American and Belgian governments that made use of Congolese accomplices and a Belgian execution squad to carry out the slaying of the leader of this infant nation in the heart of Africa that just got its independence from Belgium on 30 June 1960.

Historians, sociologists, and geopolitical pundits all agree that Congo is the most traumatized country in Africa and the world, and that of all the atrocities that Congo experienced in its abused history, Patrice Lumumba's assassination was the single cruelest act. In fact, it is rightly viewed as the country's original sin.

The assassination took place less than seven months after the independence of this territory, occupying 7.7% of the landmass of Africa. The act transformed into a stumbling block to the hopes of implementing the lofty ideals of Congolese national unity, material prosperity, democracy, economic independence, liberty, and pan-African solidarity that Lumumba had been championing. What cannot be overlooked in particular is the fact that his assassination served as a shattering blow to the hopes, dreams, and aspirations of millions of Congolese, and it disillusioned an even greater number of Africans across the continent.

The fact that one of the Soviet Union's largest universities — The Peoples' Friendship University of Russia — that was founded on February 05, 1960, got renamed "The Patrice Lumumba University" on February 22, 1961, and the fact that this institution of higher learning went on to educate close to a hundred thousand foreigners, most of them Africans, highlights the historical significance of the young African's death to Africa and the rest of the world during the Cold War.

As it turns out, the assassination's historical importance lies in a multitude of factors, of which the most relevant at the time were based on:

- the global context in which it took place (President Eisenhower authorized the assassination and the CIA carried out his abduction and transfer; the United Nations, its Secretary-General Dag Hammarskjöld, the Soviet Union and the British MI6 were involved in the tragedy; and the Belgians directed his murder and those of his two associates before later getting rid of the bodies by digging them up and dissolving them in sulfuric acid, and then grinding and scattering the bones)
- its impact on Congolese politics since then,
- and Lumumba's overall legacy as a civic-nationalist leader and pan-Africanist icon. After all, he was working with Félix Moumié, the Cameroonian liberation movement leader whom the French Secret Service (SDECE) poisoned in Geneva, Switzerland, on November 03, 1960.

One question that has been prevalent in the geopolitical sphere is this:

Why did the USA, Britain, France, and Belgium get involved in the assassination of Congo's first democratically elected leader?

It all began in April 1884, seven months before the Berlin Conference, when the United States of America became the first country in the world to recognize the claims of the Belgian King Leopold II to the territories of the Congo Basin. These territories became known as the Congo Free State. King Leopold II ruled it as his private property, making use of a small cadre of white administrators who were drawn from across Europe.

Partition Map of Africa

The Congo Free State made King Leopold II one of the wealthiest monarchs in the world, an outsized accomplishment, given the fact that he was the king of Belgium, which was such a small country in the neighborhood of mighty geopolitical entities like the British, German, Russian and Austro-Hungarian Empires. But the

Belgian king's wealth was accumulated at an enormous cost to the native African population as the people were forced to provide unpaid labor that was not different from slavery, in the exploitation of the land's mineral, forest and agricultural resources for the Belgian monarch. However, when the atrocities related to the brutal economic exploitation in King Leopold's Congo Free State resulted in millions of fatalities, the United States of America joined other world powers and forced the Belgian state to take over the Congo Free State as a regular colony and stop the killings and maiming of the native Congolese population — a genocide, per se.

It was only after Congo was transformed into a regular colony that the United States of America acquired a strategic stake in the enormous natural wealth of the territory. In fact, the USA used the uranium from Congolese mines to manufacture the first atomic weapons that were used on the Japanese cities of Hiroshima and Nagasaki, leading to an abrupt end of the Second World War in the Pacific.

The strategic importance of resource-rich Congo in particular, and resource-rich Africa in general, especially in helping the Allies win the Second World War, became a curse afterwards when the continent sought independence from its colonial masters. This was at a time when the Cold War was dominating geopolitics. America and its Western allies resolved to give the colonies independence, all right, but not the type of independence the rest of the world knew about. The Western powers were not prepared to let the people of the African colonies have effective control over the strategic raw materials in their territories, for fear that these assets could fall into the hands of the countries of the Soviet or communist camp. That was why Western interests perceived a threat in Patrice Lumumba's resolve to achieve genuine independence for Congo and to gain full control over the country's resources for use in developing the infant nation and in improving the living conditions of the Congolese people.

The Natural Resources of the Central African Region

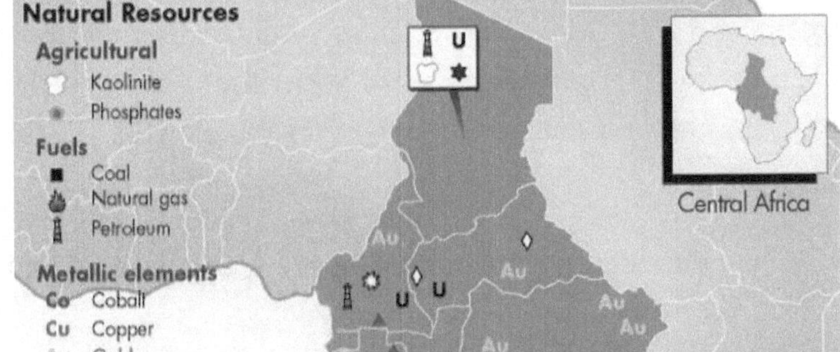

To stop Patrice Lumumba, the United States of America and Belgium left no stone unturned, including the use of the United Nations Secretariat under Dag Hammarskjöld and Ralph Bunche, the buying of the support of Lumumba's Congolese rivals, the silencing of some African leaders who had been supportive of Lumumba and the pan-Africanist goal he shared, and the buying of the services of killers for hire (mercenaries) to eliminate the obstacle to their smooth control of Congo, a country that they intended to be nothing but a quasi-independent state that is subservient to western leaders, the western countries and western interests.

Right after granting independence to Congo on June 30, 1960, Belgium and its western allies went about undermining the infant nation's stability by encouraging a virulent opposition to Lumumba's government, using western-backed Congolese politicians. In fact, by December 1960, Congo was effectively under four separate governments, three of which were under the thumbs of the anti-Lumumba factions backed by Western Powers. These were:

- the central government in the Congolese capital of Léopoldville (Kinshasa)
- a rival central government established by Lumumba's followers in Stanleyville (Kisangani)
- a secessionist regime in the mineral-rich province of Katanga under the leadership of Moise Tshombe
- and another secessionist administration in the South Kasai province under the leadership of Albert Kalonji.

With Lumumba liquidated half a year after the granting of independence to Congo, with the removal of what the Western geopolitical players perceived as the major threat to their interests in the new country, Belgium, Britain, France, and the United States of America led international efforts to spread the authority of the moderate and pro-

Western regime in Kinshasa over the entire Congo. It was a two-pronged strategy involving the use of the new Western-created Congolese army under the command of the Western-backed regime of Mobutu Sese Seko and the use of United Nations peacekeepers. The strategy was so effective that the Lumumbist stronghold in the East of the country, centered around Kisangani, fell in August 1961. South Kasai region capitulated in September 1962, and the secession of the Katanga region was reversed in January 1963.

The 1960-1961 Congo Crisis

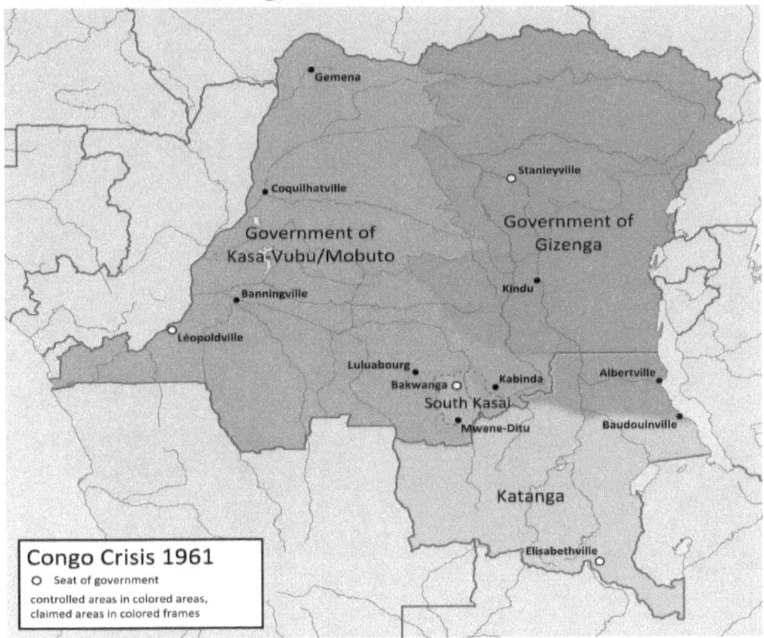

After wrecking the newly independent Congo in order to undermine Lumumba, after assassinating Lumumba and installing a puppet government, and then directing it in uniting and stabilizing the country again, the Western powers were surprised when a radical social movement for a "second independence" arose, challenging the neocolonial state and its pro-Western leadership. It was a mass movement of workers, lower civil servants, the urban unemployed, peasants, and students. They were provided leadership by Lumumba's lieutenants, most of whom had regrouped in the former French Congolese capital of Brazzaville, across the Congo River from the former Belgian Congolese capital city of Kinshasa.

The 1964 Simba Rebellion

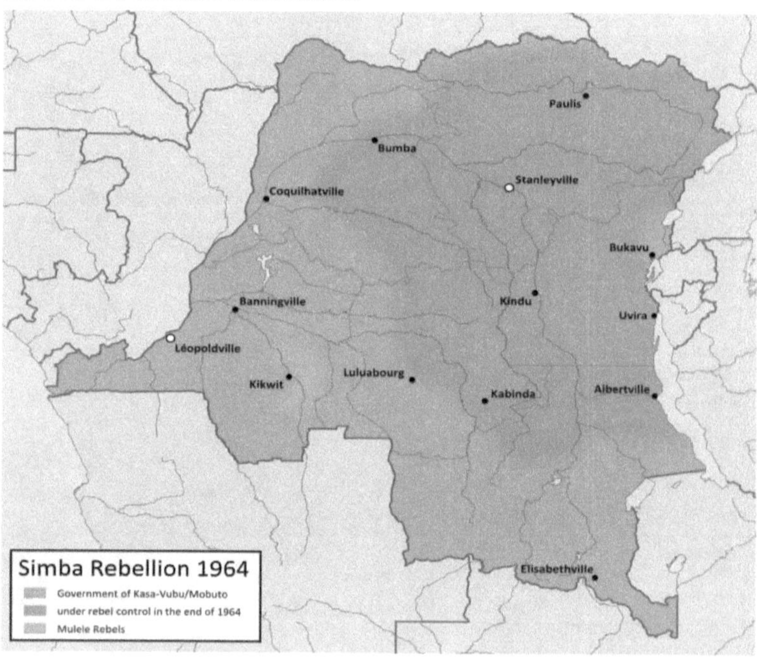

In October 1963, these Lumumbists established a National Liberation Council (CNL) with a mission to oust the

Mobutu regime and create a New Congo. They were taken seriously to the point where the Soviet Union gave them military assistance. Some of the few surviving pan-Africanist governments on the continent provided support as well. Even Ernesto Che Guevara, the Argentine revolutionary icon and second in command of Fidel Castro of Cuba, set up a base in the Congo to help these Lumumbists and anti-neocolonialists. In fact, when Che Guevara wrote in 1964 that:

"We must move forward, striking out tirelessly against imperialism. From all over the world, we have to learn lessons which events afford. Lumumba's murder should be a lesson for all of us...",

he began the immortalization of Patrice Lumumba after failing in his Congo expedition to galvanize the Lumumbists against the Western puppet regime of Mobutu Sese Seko, who not only impoverished Congo during his three-and-a-half-decade rule, but also became richer than the country he misruled.

In all the continents of the world today, streets, parks, squares, airports, statues and other infrastructures abound that bear the name Lumumba in honor of an altruist, a man who embraced a more advanced form of civic-nationalism called union-nationalism, who opposed the division of his country along ethnic or regional lines, and who supported pan-Africanism and the liberation of all the colonial territories not only in Africa, but also in the rest of the world.

Patrice Lumumba's legacy continues to serve as an inspiration in Congolese politics today, as dozens of political parties proclaim their belief in his ideas of "Positive Neutralism," which advocates a return to African values and which rejects any imported ideology, including the ideology of the Soviet Union:

"We are not Communists or Catholics. We are African nationalists," Patrice Lumumba once said.

Pan-Africanists (those who dream of a future African Economic Union with an integrated political system and military structure) cherish the Lumumba legacy and place him alongside Kwame Nkrumah of Ghana, Sekou Touré of Guinea, Julius Nyerere of Tanzania and the leaders of the historic UPC party of Cameroon — who got liquidated during their fight against French colonialism and neocolonialism that led to the country's unification and independence — as the icons of Africa's independence-struggle era that sowed the seeds for the African Union, which is yet to be realized.

On May 31, 1997, a Lumumbist made it to power after leading a full-scale rebellion against the rule of the ailing Mobutu under the banner of the Alliance of Democratic Forces for the Liberation of Congo-Zaire (ADFL), and with support from Rwanda, Uganda and Burundi, thereby marking the end of the First Congo War in a feat that took the ADFL just half a year to sweep across the country, a territory that is slightly more than half the size of the European Union. Laurent-Désiré Kabila, as Mobuto's nemesis or new president was called, made a powerful statement when he changed the name of the country from Zaire to the Democratic Republic of the Congo, which is how the central African nation was known from 1964-1971.

Laurent-Désiré Kabila did not come from nowhere. As a matter of fact, by 1965, he had emerged as the most distinguished of the late Patrice Lumumba's lieutenants following the early 1960s Congo Crisis and the rebellion against Mobutu Sese Sekou that followed it. Che Guevara even acknowledged him during his Congo expedition, even though the Argentine revolutionary thought his Congolese counterpart was too distracted at the time, concluding that he was "not the man of the hour".

Even though Laurent Kabila's former allies (Rwanda, Uganda, and Burundi) would turn against him a year later, and back a new rebellion against his rule under the banner of the of the Rally for Congolese Democracy (RCD), thereby sparking off the Second Congo War that saw him lose control of Eastern Congo, the Lumumba legacy prevailed as he held onto the south and west of the country with assistance from Angola, Namibia, and Zimbabwe. Laurent Kabila would be shot and killed by his guard on January 01, 2001, a year and a half after the withdrawal of all foreign troops from the country. The Lumumba legacy never got abandoned, though, as his son, Joseph Kabila, succeeded him and governed until January 25, 2019, when Félix Tshisekedi became the new president following his election win the year before. The Kabila team and the team of the new president hammered out a working alliance in early 2019, the result of which is a cabinet-sharing agreement between the Kabila-aligned FCC and Tshisekedi's CACH alliance, which has ensured a continuation in power of the forces that acknowledge Patrice Lumumba's positive role in Congolese history, even if they are failing to live up to the standards he upheld.

Noam Chomsky succinctly expressed the tragic nature of Patrice Lumumba's death during a September 11, 2013, interview with the renowned non-establishment broadcast journalist, syndicated columnist, investigative reporter, and author Amy Goodman, whose investigative assignments took her to places like Nigeria and East Timor, when he said the following:

"The murder of Lumumba, in which the U.S. was involved, in the Congo destroyed Africa's major hope for development. Congo is now a total horror story, for years,"

Now, Professor Noam Chomsky, who is considered by many as the greatest intellectual alive, is also respected as a great American historian, linguist, philosopher, political activist, cognitive scientist, and social critic whose mastery of analytic philosophy is enviable. So, when he continues going back to Congo to highlight the country's plight as a victim of slavery, colonialism, neocolonialism, the Cold War, imperialism, and also of globalism, we get to understand why some pundits view the geopolitical entity as the strangulated heart of Africa, whose resources seem to be a curse rather than a blessing. When he pointed out to his audience that:

"The main mineral in your cell phone, coltan [a black metallic ore], comes from the Eastern Congo. Multinational corporations are there exploiting the very rich mineral resources of the region. A lot of them are backing militias which are fighting one another to gain control of the resources or a piece of the resources."

He underscored the reason why this country that occupies most of the space that is middle or central Africa is the playground of the foreign forces that see in Africa and its rich resources nothing but booty that can be pillaged at little or no cost by eliminating those who support defending the interests of the land and the people, and then replacing them with compradors who would work for foreign interests and their own interests instead, against the interest of their countries and people.

It is hardly three decades ago that Zaire (Congo-Kinshasa) and Cameroon had the reputation for being the only two countries in Africa where those who sacrificed their lives, body parts and resources for the liberation or independence of the aforementioned countries had never governed. So the fact that Congolese of the former Belgian Congo managed to overcome their leaders with the evil disposition that were put in place by foreign powers to serve the interests of these alien powers against the welfare of the Congolese people, tells us that the country has come a long way in the difficult journey to reverse the ravages of slavery, colonialism, neocolonialism and imperialism, leaving Cameroon as the only country in Africa with an unfinished liberation that risks tearing the haunted country apart, unless the civic-nationalists of Cameroon act in a timely manner in dismantling the French-imposed system that the regime of Paul Biya manages, in what is generally the degeneration of this geopolitical entity known as the microcosm of Africa.

Democracy Index: Africa and the World

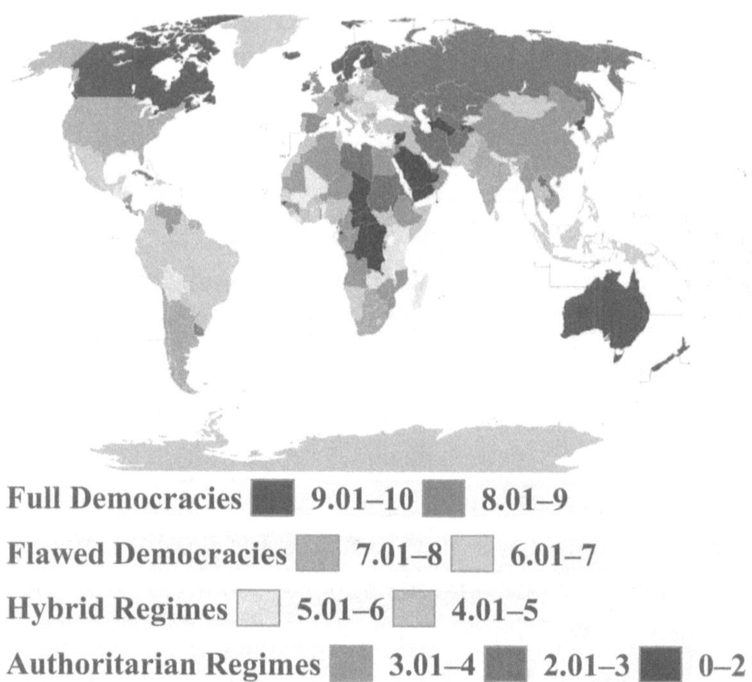

African Countries

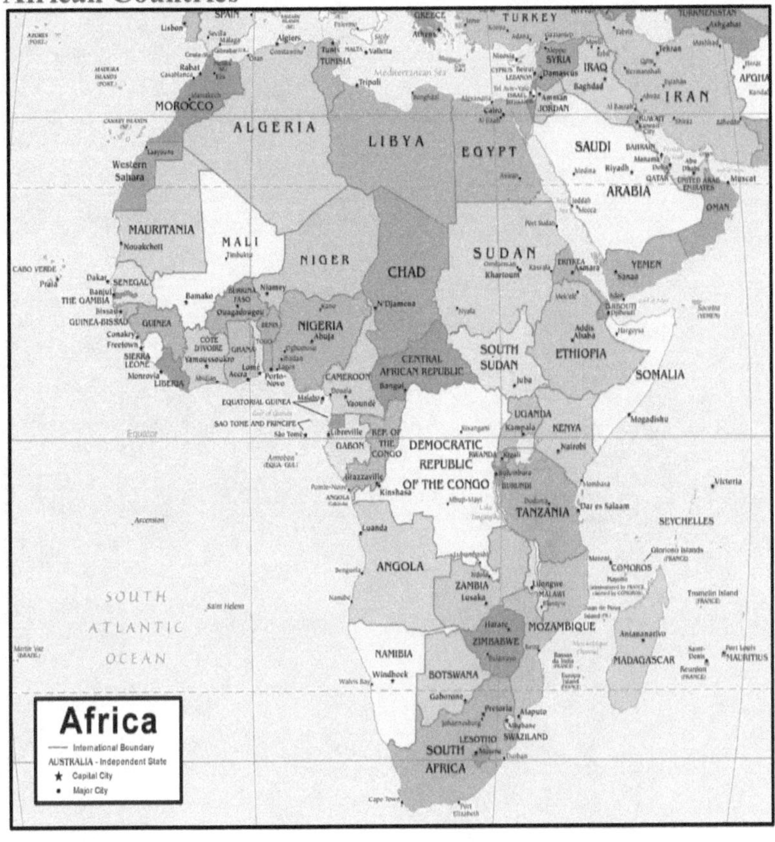

Chapter Two

Félix-Roland Moumié

QUOTES

"If we fight to the death against an arbitrary integration of our country into the French colonial empire, it is because we want to remain the conquering defenders of the right of peoples to self-determination. We are thus in the service of Kamerun and Africa...we are the true craftsmen of international detente. As revolutionary nationalists, we are fighting to realize for the Kamerun and for it alone, a true national "Independence" with "Unification" as a precondition, simultaneous or consecutive, but never excluded."

Ruben Um Nyobè

"We are not involved in this struggle only because we think that we will dismantle this system in the course of our lives. We hope Cameroon changes tomorrow. But if it doesn't, we will be happy to know that we made the ground fertile for the next generation that will end the rot in this country and then establish the 'NEW CAMEROON'."

Dr. Samuel F. Tchwenko, former UPCist and chief ideologue of the historic SDF of 1990-2002

"A people who are determined to fight for freedom and independence is invincible."

Ruben Um Nyobè

"Cameroon is not a country of slaves that no man can free."
Janvier Chouteu-Chando

"The enemy is not the one who is facing you with a sword in hand; that's the opponent. The enemy is the one behind you with a knife at your back."
Thomas Sankara

"...The world gets blessed every now and then with unique souls who, though burdened by their invisible crosses, still have the extraordinary strength to forge ahead in life and give others a helping hand at the same time. Despite their tribulations, most of us think they are fine. Even when the weight of their crosses become unbearable, even when they proceed in a breathless manner, we still have a hard time understanding that they are drowning. In fact, we even condemn them for failing to sacrifice more..."
Janvier Chouteu-Chando, Disciples of Fortune

"Political independence has no meaning if it is not accompanied by rapid economic and social development."
Patrice Lumumba

"The worst thing that colonialism did was to cloud our view of our past."
Barack Obama

"Until the lions have their own historians, the history of the hunt will always glorify the hunter."
Chinua Achebe

"The characters in our other lives are ghosts that literature is reviving."
Olivier Weber

Cameroon on a map of the world

Countries on the Map of Africa

Cameroon over time

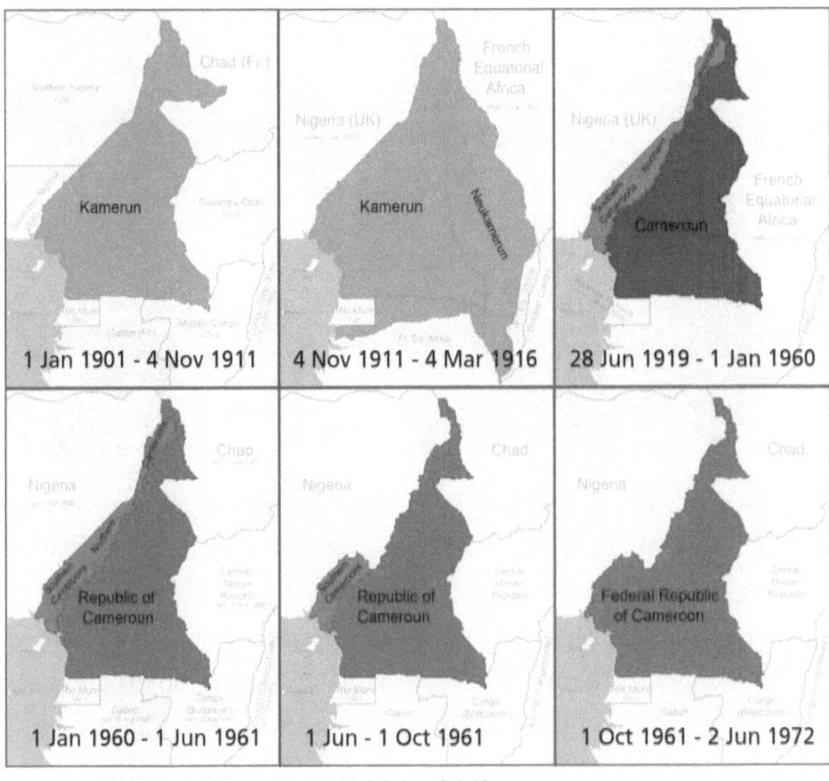

1. German Kamerun (1884-1911)
2. German Kamerun (1911-1916)
3. British Cameroons & French Cameroun: 1916-1960
4. British Cameroons & La Republique du Cameroun (1960-1961)
5. British Southern Cameroons & La Republique du Cameroun (1960-1961)
6. Reunited/Independent Cameroon today.

UPC Leaders (L. to R.) front row: Castor Osendé Afana, Abel Kingué, Ruben Um Nyobé, Félix Moumié, and Ernest Ouandié

Born in 1926, Félix-Roland Moumié was an anti-colonialist Cameroonian leader and Pan-Africanist. His assassination in Geneva on November 03, 1960, by William Bechtel of the SDECE (the French Secret Service) with thallium is regarded as the most brazen crime committed by the French secret service abroad, and perhaps the biggest single blow suffered by Cameroonian civic-nationalists fighting for the liberation of the land from French neocolonial control.

Dr. Felix-Roland Moumié was the head of the UPC (*Union des Populations du Cameroun,* also called *Union du Peuple Camerounais* — "Union of the Populations of Cameroon") from 1958 to 1960. The UPC was the first historic political party to emerge from the territories of the former German colony of Kamerun. Founded in 1948, the UPC operated in both French Cameroun and British Cameroons — Trust Territories that emerged from the 1884-1916 former German Kamerun following its partition between Britain and France as agreed in the June 28, 1919 Treaty of Versailles, the most important of the peace treaties that brought World War I to a close, by formalizing the end of the state of war between Germany and the Allied Powers. The party's primary objective was the reunification and independence of British Cameroons and French Cameroun, Trust Territories that were the successors of the League of Nations mandates, and that came into being when the League of Nations ceased to exist in 1946.

Cameroon over time

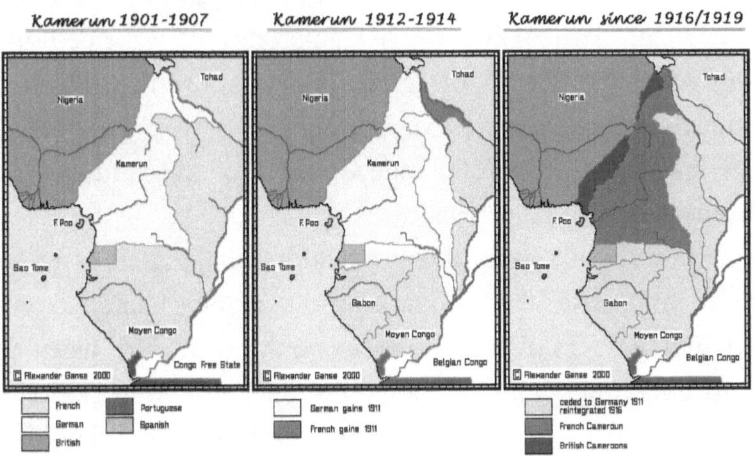

The French Trusteeship administration banned the UPC in 1955, accusing it of fomenting civil unrest, thereby forcing the party into exile in the summer of 1955. However, the UPC resurfaced in 1956 and challenged France via international media. The British colonial authorities also banned the UPC in British Cameroons in 1958, thereby forcing most of its leadership that escaped French Cameroun and sought sanctuary in British Cameroons, to flee to Egypt, Ghana, China, and other countries that were supportive of the Cameroonian cause for its reunification and independence.

Ruben Um Nyobé, the party's leader and Secretary-General; Ernest Ouandié and Abel Kingué, the party's two vice presidents; and Felix Moumié pledged to carry on with the struggle for the reunification and independence of French Cameroun and British Cameroons, despite France's resolve to divide and rule the peoples of the former German Kamerun. After all, the UPC commanded the support of most of the people of French Cameroun, and its offshoots and sister parties in British Cameroons commanded the support of the electorate there. In fact, more than 80% of educated Cameroonians supported the party and its cause for the reunification and independence of the lands of the former German Kamerun.

However, the party received its first major trauma when three years after the ban, at a time that some pundits were beginning to think that France would allow the party to start operating again as a legal political entity, the security forces of the French Trusteeship administration assassinated the UPC's first historic leader Ruben Um Nyobé on September 13, 1958, near his home village of Boumnyebel in the Bassaland.

So, when Dr. Felix-Roland Moumié succeeded Ruben Um Nyobé, he was forced to operate from exile, even though the UPC was the only party in French Cameroun that enjoyed the overwhelming support of French Camerounians, and even though it was also the only political party in that part of the former German Kamerun that shared a similar program with sister parties or offshoots in British Cameroons. Undeterred, he challenged

France's crackdown on the UPC in a more determined manner, so that UPC partisans were in control of much the countryside of the southern half of French Cameroun before France handed French Cameroun's political control or sovereignty to its puppet Ahmadou Ahidjo, declared the land independent on January 01, 1960, and at the same time concluded a series of socio-economic and political agreements with the infant state that virtually made it a backyard of France.

The Years African Countries were given their independence by their Colonial Masters.

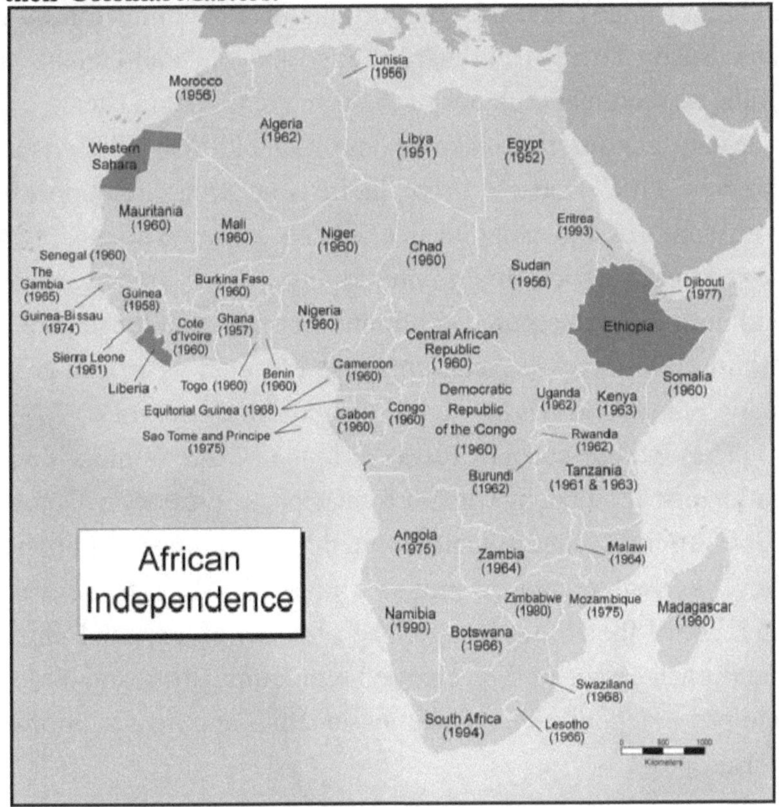

Considered by some as the "African Che Guevara in the making", Félix Moumié was an astute leader as well as a great organizer who, before his death, had met that summer of 1960 with Ernesto Che Guevara, the Argentine international revolutionary and second-in-command in the new anti-American and anti-Western government of Fidel Castro's Cuba. In addition to that development, the Cameroonian partisan leader had successfully developed a special rapport with the bellicose Egyptian president Gamal Abdel Nasser, the Pan-Africanist president of Ghana Kwame Nkrumah, the unwavering Patrice Lumumba of Congo-Kinshasa (the former Belgian Congo), and the stubborn nationalist Guinean head of state Sékou Touré who defied France and whisked Guinea out of the neocolonial clutches of its former colonial master.

Many pundits think France and its Cold War allies feared the new UPC leader's drive in forging strong relationships with some of the other leaders in the communist bloc, who hoped to see Africa emerge one day as an economically united and politically integrated continent. The fact that those leaders promised to increase their support to Moumié's partisan group made France and Ahmadou Ahidjo extremely nervous.

The exiled second leader of the Cameroonian civic-nationalist movement was on a mission to Europe in October 1960, when William Bechtel invited him to dinner in a hotel in Geneva, Switzerland, posing as a journalist. In fact, he was a member of the "Main Rouge," an offshoot of a special unit in the French secret service charged with eliminating anti-French and pro-independence African nationalists and their supporters in Europe.

Distracted by a summons to the phone by a restaurant staff,

Moumié left his unfinished drink, which Bechtel contaminated by pouring a lethal dose of thallium into it. But Moumié did not drink it upon his return. So, Bechtel created another distraction, during which he poured another dose of thallium into Moumié's wine. Moumié ended up gulping down both drinks and died in a Geneva hospital on November 3, 1960, days before his return to Guinea, and much earlier than his killers had planned. The fact that the Cameroonian liberation leader took an overdose of the poison thwarted the plot France had hatched to blame Felix Moumié's death on Guinean president Sekou Touré, who had been acting as the UPC leader's host during his exile in the Guinean capital of Conakry.

The Body of Félix Moumié is Flown to Guinea for Burial

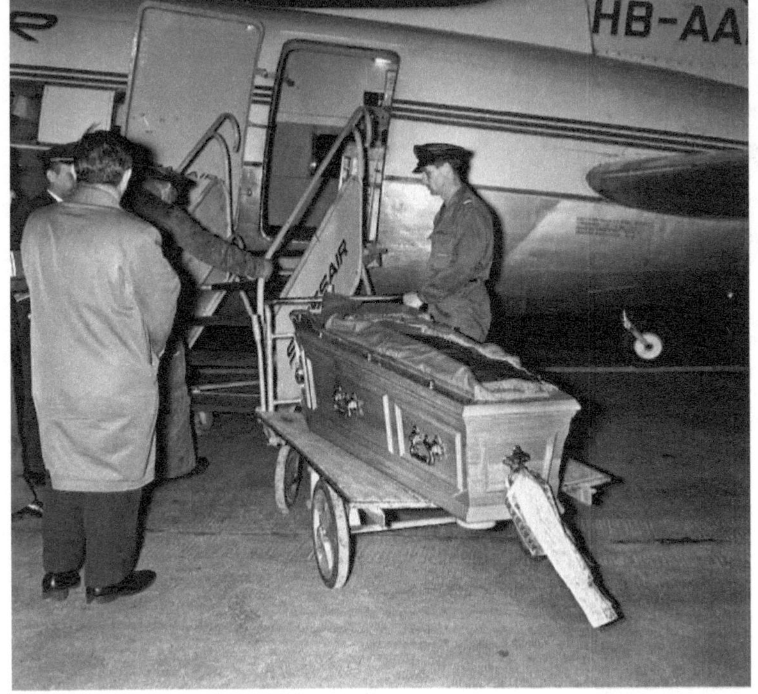

Félix Moumié's assassination would be followed three months later by the horrendous assassination of Patrice Lumumba of the former Belgian Congo. The deaths of these two African civic-nationalists with a Pan-Africanist vision would be followed by a bloody repression of the popular resistance to the neo-colonial regimes in their respective countries.

With the execution of Félix Moumié's successor, Ernest Ouandie, in January 1971, the neo-colonial counter-offensive against the anti-colonialist movements in the heart of Africa would be over, spelling victory for the neo-colonial forces. This new reality would have disastrous consequences not only in the Central African region but throughout Africa. Francophone Sub-Saharan Africa has not dared to oppose French neocolonialism since the defeat of Cameroonian civic-nationalism and France's imposition of a mafia-like system of control over its former colonies that makes use of French puppets who are not accountable to their people.

Partition Map of Africa

The death of Félix Moumié, the retention of the French ban on the UPC, the UPC's 1958 expulsion from British Cameroons, and the return to power in France of the French legend and neocolonialist General Charles De Gaulle made the realization of the Kamerunian dream of reunification, independence and development seem impossible. However, offshoots of the UPC in British Cameroons and the Cameroonian civic-nationalists in British Southern Cameroons realized the reunification dream by championing the campaign in the United Nations-sponsored plebiscite or referendum for the vote to reunite British Southern Cameroons with the one-year-old Republic of Cameroun, the former French Cameroun that got its independence on January 01, 1960, under the anti-UPC government of the French puppet Ahmadou Ahidjo.

Cameroon's Journey to Independence and Reunification

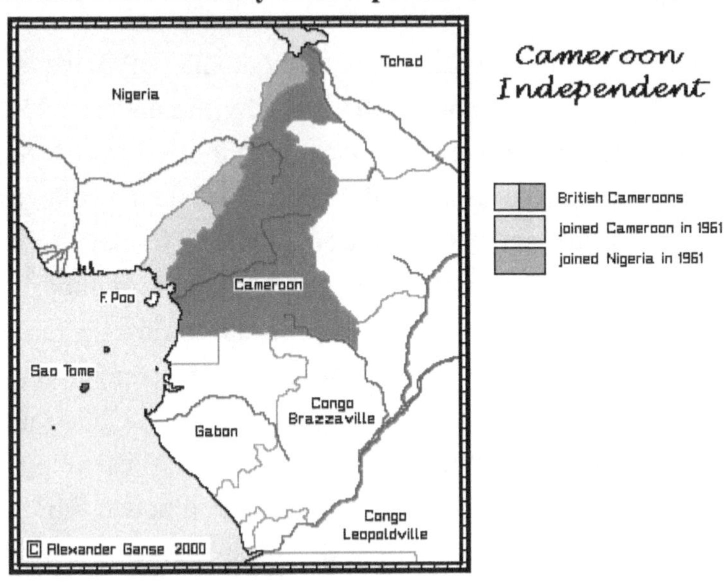

11-12 February 1961 British Cameroons Plebiscite
Main Points: Voters were asked if they wanted to unite with Nigeria or Cameroon when independence is granted to the two regions.
Northern Cameroons
Registered Voters   292,985
Total Votes (Voter   Not Available (N/A)
Turnout)
Invalid/Blank Votes   Not Available
Total Valid Votes   243,955
Southern Cameroons
Registered Voters   349,652
Total Votes (Voter   Not Available (N/A)
Turnout)
Invalid/Blank Votes   Not Available
Total Valid Votes   331,312

Results	Northern Cameroons		Southern Cameroons	
	Number of Votes	% of Votes	Number of Votes	% of Votes
Union with the Federation of Nigeria	146,296	59.97%	97,741	29.50%
Union with the Republic of Cameroon	97,659	40.03%	233,571	70.50%

In fact, even though inferiorly armed, the UPC led an effective guerrilla campaign that had, by the end of 1959, confined complete French control in the south of the country only to the cities and towns, leaving the villages and countryside under the control of the UPC. And since the UN Trusteeship Agreement set a cap on the number of troops the French Army could have in the territory, France decided to precipitate the granting of independence to French Cameroon. However, it granted French Cameroun independence on January 01, 1960, under its puppet Ahmadou Ahidjo, and at the same time compelled Ahidjo to sign a secretive pact with France, an agreement with economic, political and military components that among other things, allowed France to multiply the number of French troops it had stationed in the former French Cameroun, called the Republic of Cameroon thereafter. The French army would reinforce its presence in the land by increasing the number of its soldiers and hardware there, and by speeding up the recruitment and training of a French-led local Cameroonian Army. These Franco-Cameroonian armies would defeat the insurgents in its major strongholds in the Bassaland in 1960 and in the Bamilekeland from 1962-1964, by inflicting heavy losses on the UPC and the civilian populations through their indiscriminate bombing of both the guerilla camps and the civil communities, a scorched-earth policy per se that some historians and various pundits consider a French-led genocide against certain forces and populations of areas of Cameroon that opposed France's neocolonialist plans for Cameroon.

The UPC realized by 1965 that it could no longer win the armed conflict against the French Army and the Cameroonian Army that France created for the puppet Ahmadou Ahidjo regime. Prevaricated efforts at achieving peace through peace talks would lure Felix Moumié's successor Ernest Ouandie out of the bush, leading to his surrender/capture, and then execution in January 1971, thereby ending the UPC armed struggle against France for the reunification, independence and freedom of the territories of the former German Kamerun, a conflict that resulted in the deaths of more than half a million Cameroonian lives in what some pundits view as

"Cameroon's Unfinished Liberation", since those and the heirs of those who campaigned and fought for Cameroon's reunification and independence have been prevented from power in the country ever since.

Cameroonians from the English-speaking part of the reunited Cameroon soon realized that they had been deceived and subjugated by France and her puppet, like the defeated and subdued populations of the French-speaking part of the country, and that they too were now under the suffocating yoke of a French-imposed system managed by the dictatorship of France's puppet, Ahmadou Ahidjo. Paul Biya, another French marionette and Ahmadou Ahidjo's successor from the orders of France, has been in power since 1982 and has exacerbated the suffocation of Cameroon even further. Close to sixty years after, Cameroon is still under the control of the anti-UPC forces put in place by France — these are Cameroonians who played no role, whether as moderates or as radicals, in the nationalist struggle for the land's reunification and independence. In fact, France aided its puppets in establishing a police state to impose their rule, which explains why Cameroon has never experienced rule under a head of state that is or was the choice of the people.

The mafia continues. The country that embodies Africa's daring spirit is still in the grips of the forces that were against its quest for liberation, development, and partnership with other progressive forces of the world.

The assassinations of Ruben Um Nyobé, Félix Moumié, Patrice Lumumba, Castor Osendé Afana, Ernest Ouandie and tens of thousands of Congolese and Cameroonian civic-nationalists were, after all, a successful campaign by neocolonial powers to destroy Africa's genuine independent development, as defeating the anti-colonial movements in these countries weakened the pan-Africanist drive to create an African economic union and to integrate the continent politically. Despite indications or expectations to the contrary, the Cameroon of Nyobè/Moumié/Ouandie that was never realized, and the Congo of Lumumba that failed to be, would have been at the geographic, economic and political center of the African Union that is still the vision for many progressive Africans who hope to see the continent secure a place of respect for itself in the growing multi-polar world.

Today, Félix Moumié's sarcophagus is still missing in what was his resting place in the cemetery in Conakry, Guinea. Albert Kingue is still buried in Cairo, Egypt. Ruben Um Nyobé, Ernest Ouandie, Castor Osendé Afana, and the other leaders of the UPC killed by the Franco-Ahidjo forces are hardly acknowledged, let alone recognized in the annals of Cameroonian history, even though their names grace streets and infrastructures in other countries of Africa and the world.

Six decades later, Cameroonians rising to challenge the mafia state still see Felix-Roland Moumié and the other historic Union-Nationalist leaders that got killed, exiled, or undermined by France and the puppets it imposed on the country, as the forces to emulate in their drive to dismantle the system imposed on the people. The system and its authoritarian political establishment are led today by Paul Biya, a puppet imposed by France on the people of

Cameroon. The second Cameroonian president has been in power for forty-seven years (thirty-seven years as the president or head of state since 1982, and ten years as prime minister of the only country in Africa where its head of state has never been the choice of the people, but rather an imposition by neocolonialists).

Democracy Index: Africa and the World

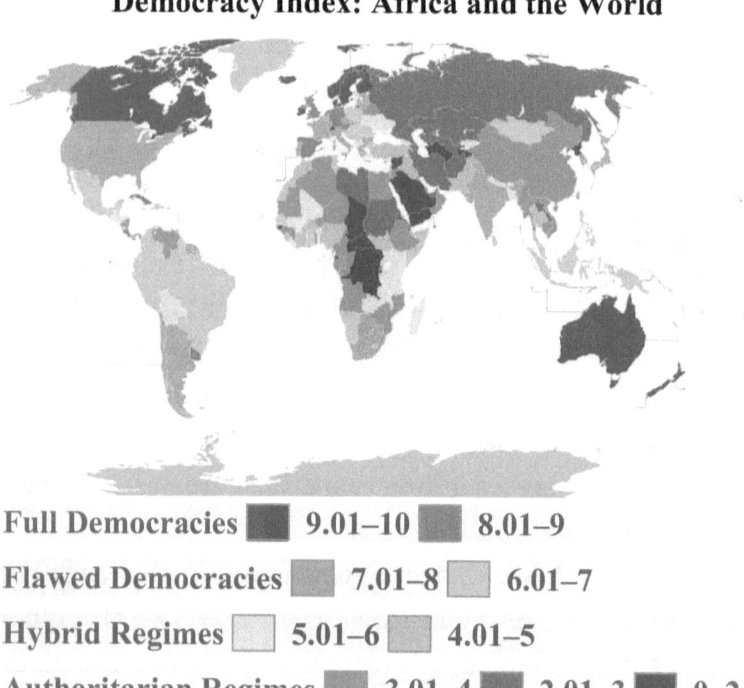

African Countries

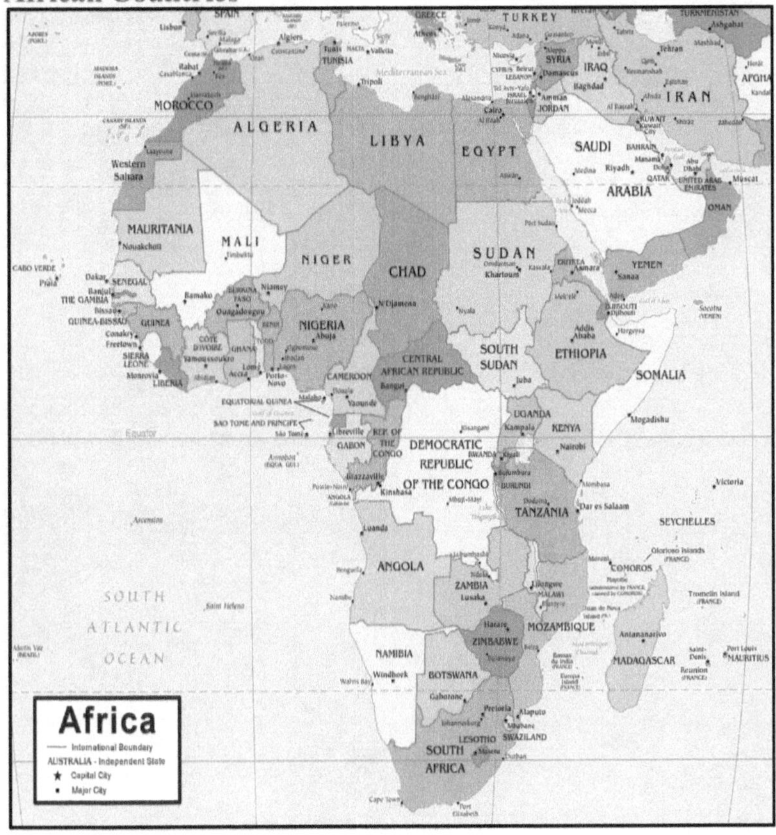

Chapter Three

Thomas Sankara

QUOTES FROM THOMAS SANKARA

"While revolutionaries as individuals can be murdered, you cannot kill ideas."

"The enemy is not the one who is facing you with a sword in hand; that's the opponent. The enemy is the one behind you with a knife at your back."

"Without patriotic political education, a soldier is only a potential criminal."

"I do not think that Blaise (Blaise Compaoré, his deputy and best friend) wants to make an attempt on my life. The only danger is that if he refuses to act, the imperialist powers will offer him power on a silver platter by organizing my assassination. Even if they succeed in assassinating me, it does not matter! The bottom line is that they want to eat, and I am stopping them. But I shall die peacefully, for never, after what we have succeeded in instilling in the consciences of our countrymen, they cannot control our people as formerly."

"The greatest difficulty we have faced is the neocolonial way of thinking that exists in this country. We were colonized by a country, France, which left us with certain habits. For us, being successful in life, being happy, meant trying to live as they do in France, like the richest of the French."

"You cannot carry out fundamental change without a certain amount of madness. In this case, it comes from nonconformity, the courage to turn your back on the old formulas, the courage to invent the future."

"Debt is a cleverly managed reconquest of Africa. It is a reconquest that turns each one of us into a financial slave."

"Let there be an end to the arrogance of the big powers who miss no opportunity to put the rights of the people in question. Africa's absence from the club of those who have the right to veto is unjust and should be ended."

"We are not against progress, but we do not want progress that is anarchic and criminally neglects the rights of others."

"Inequality can be done away with only by establishing a new society, where men and women will enjoy equal rights...Thus, the status of women will improve only with the elimination of the system that exploits them."

"The spirit is smothered, as it were, by ignorance, but as soon as ignorance is destroyed, the spirit shines forth like the sun when it breaks through clouds."

"The patriarchal family made its appearance, founded on the sole and personal property of the father, who had become head of the family. Within this family, the woman was oppressed."

"I want people to remember me as someone whose life has been helpful to humanity."

"Our country produces enough to feed us all. Alas, for lack of organization, we are forced to beg for food aid. It's this aid that instills in our spirits the attitude of beggars."

"Everything that man can imagine, he is capable of creating."

"It took the madmen of yesterday for us to be able to act with extreme clarity today. I want to be one of those madmen. We must dare to invent the future."

"If you take a walk around Ouagadougou and make a list of the mansions you see, you will note that they belong to just a minority. How many of you who have been assigned to Ouagadougou from the farthest corners of the country have had to move every night because you've been thrown out of the house you have rented? To those who have acquired houses and land through corruption, we say: start to tremble. If you have stolen, tremble, because we will come after you."

"We must dare to invent the future."

"Women hold up the other half of the sky."

"We make every effort to see that our actions live up to our words and be vigilant with regard to our behavior."

"Comrades, there is no true social revolution without the liberation of women."

"It's really a pity that there are observers who view political events like comic strips. There has to be a Zorro, there has to be a star. No, the problem of Upper Volta is more serious than that. It was a grave mistake to have looked for a man, a star, at all costs, to the point of creating one, that is, to the point of attributing the ownership of the event to Captain Sankara, who must have been the brains, etc."

"Our revolution in Burkina Faso draws on the totality of man's experiences since the first breath of humanity. We wish to be the heirs of all the revolutions of the world, of all the liberation struggles of the peoples of the Third World. We draw the lessons of the American Revolution."

"The Revolution Cannot Triumph Without the Emancipation of Women."

"The revolution and women's liberation go together. We do not talk of women's emancipation as an act of charity or out of a surge of human compassion. It is a basic necessity for the revolution to triumph. Women hold up the other half of the sky."

"Imperialism is a system of exploitation that occurs not only in the brutal form of those who come with guns to conquer territory. Imperialism often occurs in more subtle forms, a loans, food aid, and blackmail. We are fighting this system that allows a handful of men on earth to rule all of humanity."

"We have to work at decolonizing our mentality and achieving happiness within the limits of sacrifice we should be willing to make. We have to recondition our people to accept themselves as they are, to not be ashamed of their real situation, to be satisfied with it, to glory in it, even."

"The enemies of a people are those who keep them in ignorance."

"The French Revolution taught us the rights of man."

"Comrades, there is no true social revolution without the liberation of women. May my eyes never see and my feet never take me to a society where half the people are held in silence. I hear the roar of women's silence. I sense the rumble of their storm and feel the fury of their revolt."

"We must learn to live the African way. It's the only way to live in freedom and with dignity."

"He who feeds you controls you."

"Under its current form, that is imperialism-controlled, debt is a cleverly managed reconquest of Africa, aiming at subjugating its growth and development through foreign rules. Thus, each one of us becomes the financial slave, which is to say a true slave."

"May my eyes never see, and my feet never take me to a society where half the people are held in silence."

"He who does not feed you can demand nothing of you."

"Inequality can be done away with only by establishing a new society, where men and women will enjoy equal rights, resulting from an upheaval in the means of production and in all social relations. Thus, the status of women will improve only with the elimination of the system that exploits them."

"Che Guevara taught us we could dare to have confidence in ourselves, confidence in our abilities. He instilled in us the conviction that struggle is our only recourse. He was a citizen of the free world that, together, we are in the process of building. That is why we say that Che Guevara is also African and Burkinabè."

"Never be ashamed of being Afrikan."

"When the people stand up, imperialism trembles."

Burkina Faso on a Map of the World

Partition map of Africa (1884-1914)

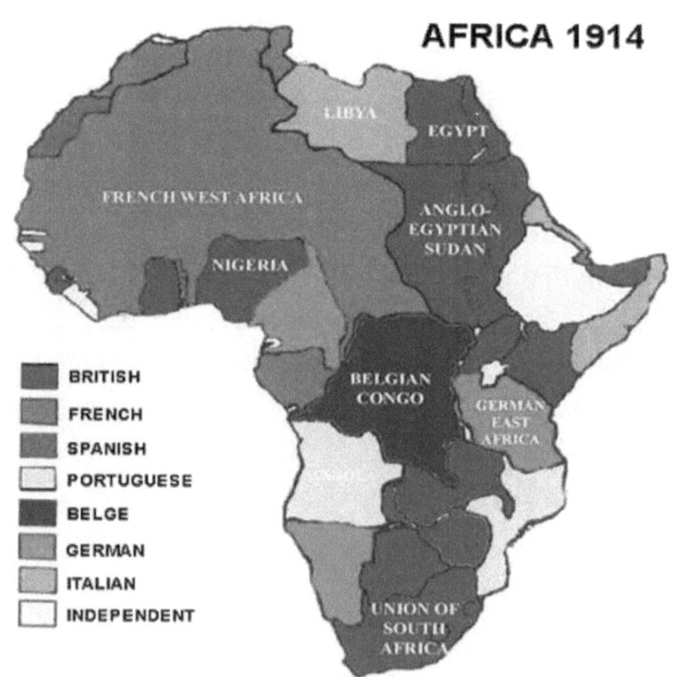

When Africa woke up that morning of October 16, 1987, and learned of the death of Thomas Sankara, the charismatic head of state of Burkina Faso, shock, grief, and melancholy settled over the continent. When more news sipped in reporting that he was killed along with twelve others in a military coup d'état led by the then Vice President Blaise Compaoré (who, after the coup, became the president and ruled until his ouster in a popular uprising on October 31, 2014), the Burkina Faso masses were outraged. Thomas Sankara had made known to the world that Blaise Compaoré was his chum and closest confidant.

So, who was this young man who took a landlocked country in Africa out of an impasse, a territory that was the heartland of the Songhai Empire, and then showed the people there and their brethren in the rest of Africa the path to a future devoid of the retarding influence of neocolonialism?

The story begins in 1949, with the birth of Thomas Sankara on December 21 of that year in Yako, Upper Volta, and became legendary with his death on Oct 15, 1987, in Ouagadougou, Burkina Faso, from the bullets of his assassins. However, we shall deal with the chapters that constitute his life on earth as we delve deeper into how he became the leader of the Burkinabe Revolution before his untimely death.

Sankara's rise to the highest office of the land began

following his training as a pilot and after he became a captain in the Upper Volta Air Force. But it wasn't only his skills as a pilot that made him a popular figure in the country's capital city called Ouagadougou, especially after fighting in the 1974 border war against Mali. The fact that he was a decent guitarist and the fact that he liked motorbikes may also have contributed to his charisma. So, his appointment as Secretary of State for Information in 1981 by Colonel Saye Zerbo, who became the president of the country after ending the 14-year rule of Sangoulé Lamizana with a coup d'état on 25 November 1980, was welcomed by the country folks. However, when Sankara resigned from the government on 21 April 1982, citing the regime's anti-labor drift, the population saw another laudable side of his character that was uncommon around. He was incorruptible.

The November 07, 1982, coup d'état led by Maj. Dr. Jean-Baptiste Ouédraogo and the Council of Popular Salvation (CSP) that overthrew Colonel Saye Zerbo brought about the resuscitation of Sankara's fortunes when the new president made him Prime Minister in 1983. But then, Jean-Christophe Mitterrand, the son of French President Francois Mitterrand, who happened to be his father's African Affairs adviser, visited Upper Volta that year, did not like the young Sankara's political ideas, bluntness, and incorruptible nature, and so made the Upper Voltan president place Sankara and some of his close associates under house arrest. His confinement by the authorities triggered a popular uprising that could not be contained.

The Sankara saga would not have taken new dimensions had a group of men in Upper Volta, known today as Burkina Faso, not decided to launch a revolution that would enable the country "to accept the responsibility of its reality and its destiny with human dignity". A coup d'état organized by Blaise Compaoré with the help of Captain Henri Bongo, Major Jean-Baptiste Booker Lingam, and the charismatic Captain Thomas Sankara deposed Jean-Baptiste Ouedraogo on 4 August 1983, after which they pronounced Thomas Sankara the leader. The 33-year-old Sankara went on to become a prominent figure in the group of African leaders who wanted to give the continent in general, and their countries in particular, a new socio-political dimension devoid of the shackles of neocolonialism, especially the overbearing French control of its former African colonies and territories.

Colonization of Africa and Dates of Independence

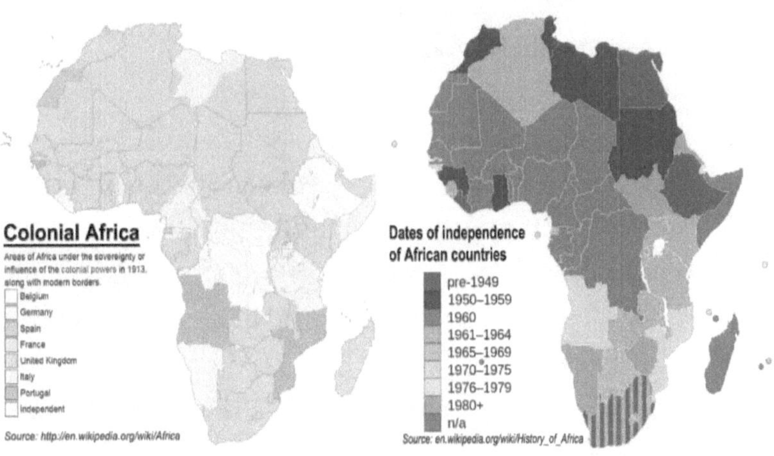

Thomas Sankara, the charismatic left-leaning leader of a country in the heart of West Africa, was sometimes nicknamed "Tom Sank" and was considered by some of his admirers as an "African Che Guevara" even before he became the head of state of the country following the coup masterminded by his friend Blaise Compaoré.

A year after assuming the highest office in the land, Sankara began the most ambitious programs for social and economic change ever attempted in any of the countries on the African continent. He changed the name of the country from Upper Volta to Burkina Faso, meaning "the land of upright people" in Mossi and Dyula, which are the country's two major languages. He also came up with a new flag and a new anthem for the enthusiastic country.

The young president would orient the country's policy towards fighting corruption, reforestation, averting famine, and towards making education and healthcare real priorities for the nation.

His domestic policies focused on:

- preventing famine with agrarian self-sufficiency and land reform that resulted in food self-sufficiency three years into his presidency
- making education a priority, which the government was relentless in pursuing through a nationwide literacy campaign
- and promoting public health by vaccinating 2,500,000 (2.5 million) children against meningitis, yellow fever, and measles.

Other laudable aspects of his national agenda included:
- The planting of over 10,000,000 (ten million) trees, which went a long way in halting the growing desertification of the Sahel
- The doubling of wheat production by redistributing land from feudal landlords to peasants
- The suspension of rural poll taxes and domestic rents
- and the launch of an ambitious road and railway construction program to "tie the nation together".

At the local level, Sankara also led the drive for every village to build a medical dispensary, and for over 350 communities to build schools using their own labor.

Right after he came to power, he became the champion of women's emancipation and rights in Africa. In fact, this was confirmed by his ban on female genital mutilation; his abolition of forced marriages, child marriages and polygamy; as well as by his policies and efforts encouraging women to take up leadership positions in the government and society, especially by appointing women to high governmental positions, and encouraging them to work outside the home and to stay in school, even if they became pregnant. When he wrote that:

"The revolution and women's liberation go together.
We do not talk of women's emancipation as an act of
charity or because of a surge of human compassion.
It is a basic necessity for the triumph of the

revolution. Women hold up the other half of the sky."

It was a reflection of his determination to improve the wellbeing of women in his country and Africa.

Sankara and Fidel Castro of Cuba

Sankara pursued a foreign policy that did not condone imperialism and that encouraged cooperation based on respect and the recognition of Burkina Faso's interests as well as the interests of the other parties dealing with Burkina Faso. This saw his government eschewing all foreign aid, pushing for debt reduction in an audacious manner, and nationalizing all land and mineral wealth, thereby averting the power and influence of the International Monetary Fund (IMF) and its sister financial institution, the World Bank.

Being one of the poorest countries in the world at the time, Burkina Faso was expected to continue kowtowing to its former colonial master and the international financial institutions. But Sankara was different. He was firmly convinced that the country could come around and sustain itself without foreign aid. He even went as far as refusing aid packages from the International Monetary Fund, which it gave with conditions attached to them that compromised Burkina Faso's sovereignty, as he saw it. He articulated this independence stance through numerous writings, speeches, interviews, and other exchanges. But at a period just after the independence of the 1960s, when most of the continent's revolutionary, pan-Africanist and daring leaders had been killed, overthrown, and cowed or humbled by threats, sanctions, sabotage, and other active measures, Sankara came across as a voice that was not being heeded. He thought he found a forum to sell his crusade at the July 1987 summit of the Organization of African Unity, where he tried to persuade the heads of state of other African countries to act collectively and not pay their financial debts to their former colonizers, pointing out that:

> *"The origins of debt go back to colonialism's origins...We cannot repay the debt because we are not responsible for this debt. On the contrary, others owe us something that no money can pay for. That is to say, the debt of blood..."*

Even though Sankara's revolutionary programs for self-reliance transformed him into an icon in the eyes of many of Africa's poor and increased his popularity with most of the impoverished citizens of Burkina Faso, his policies undermined the vested interests of a wide range of groups (the Francophile Burkinabe middle-class, the tribal leaders who resented the fact that he stripped them of their long-held traditional privileges to forced labor and payment of tributes, and France and its ally the Ivory Coast under Félix Houphouet-Boigny, whom he considered a puppet of France). So, when Blaise Compaoré orchestrated his overthrow and assassination on 15 October 1987, many people (Burkinabes and non-Burkinabes) were left wondering whether he had not seen it coming. After all, a week before his assassination, he had declared that:

"While revolutionaries as individuals can be murdered, you cannot kill ideas."

His intuition was in play all right, but he did not seem to be the type who was prepared to go through the horrors of investigating and eliminating those he had been working closely with. He, like many great figures in history, understood that betrayal from those close to you is not your fault, especially if you, as the leader, never harbored evil intentions against your associates or comrades. In fact, he had a speech with him on the morning of his death that he had prepared the night before, aimed at bridging the ideological rifts that were growing between the feuding factions in his government. An excerpt of it reads thus: *"Whatever the contradictions, whatever the oppositions, solutions will be found as long as confidence reigns…"* But he did not get to read that speech in the council meeting that morning because machine gun shots interrupted the proceedings just before it started, followed by shouts ordering everyone out. He let his fear-stricken ministers know that he was the one the gunmen were after, ordered them to stay put, raised his hands in the air, and then walked out to find his bodyguards lying dead on the stairs. Just then, the squad of attacking soldiers opened fire on him.

When the news of Thomas Sankara's assassination on October 15, 1987, went out shortly after he and twelve other officials were killed in a coup d'état organized by his former colleague Blaise Compaoré, it was received with outrage, sadness, apprehension, and disbelief in all of the countries of the world. But nowhere was the grief as great as in Burkina Faso and the rest of Africa, where he was regarded by the masses as the beacon of hope in a continent dominated by leaders with evil dispositions, most of whom were puppets of foreign powers. Blaise Compaoré not only made sure Sankara got buried in an unmarked grave, but he also desecrated Sankara's legacy even further by reversing most of his policies and by realigning Burkina Faso with those foreign leaders and countries that were hostile to Sankara, especially the former colonial master, France. Many people versed in history wasted no time comparing Blaise Compaoré to Brutus (Marcus Julius Brutus), a politician of the Roman Republic who participated in the assassination of his close friend, the Roman Emperor Julius Caesar.

The fact that Blaise Compare would have Henri Zongo

and Jean-Baptiste Boukary Lingani, whom he had initially been ruling with in a triumvirate, arrested, charged with plotting to overthrow the government, summarily tried, and then executed in September 1989, proved that Sankara was a trusting and trusted member in that group that seized power in 1983 and began the Burkinabe Revolution.

Sankara's quest to realize the most ambitious programs for social and economic change ever attempted on the African continent ended up as a partially realized dream, but it was a vision that is appreciated for stirring the hopes of the African youth. Today, he is a legend in his country and Africa, three decades after his death.

Antonio de Figueiredo, a journalist, activist and broadcaster who campaigned for the liberation of Portugal's African colonies, and who did more than anyone to bring the issue of colonial oppression in Angola, Mozambique, Guinea and Cape Verde to the attention of the English-speaking world, understood the magnitude of Thomas Sankara's influence when he wrote in February 2008 that:

> *"Africa and the world are yet to recover from Sankara's assassination. Just as we have yet to recover from the loss of Patrice Lumumba, Kwame Nkrumah, Eduardo Mondlane, Amílcar Cabral, Steve Biko, Samora Machel, and, most recently, John Garang, to name only a few. While malevolent forces have not used the same methods to eliminate each of these great pan-Africanists, they have been guided by the same motive: to keep Africa in chains."*

Thomas Sankara, the revolutionary and short-lived head of state of Burkina Faso who reduced his salary to 450 US Dollars, sold the government's fleet of Mercedes Benz cars, banned the allocation of chauffeurs for government officials and made the Renault 5 the official car, was commemorated in ceremonies that took place in Burkina Faso, Mali, Senegal, Niger, Tanzania, Burundi, France, Canada, and the United States of America on 15 October 2007, twenty years after his assassination. The sorely missed African legend that got eliminated from the geopolitical arena by the neocolonial forces of this world and their African puppets and compradors, just as he was beginning to stir the dream of Pan-Africanism again, was exhumed in 2015 following a request by his family.

The exhumation took place one year after the popular uprising that forced Blaise Compaoré out of power and compelled him to flee Burkina Faso into exile in the neighboring Ivory Coast. Public anger against Blaise Compaore that had been building since the assassination of Sankara in 1987 spilled over into the streets after Compaore's 2014 attempt to change the constitution that would have allowed him to run for office again for the fifth time and for two more terms in what is generally considered election masquerades — a trend seen in authoritarian and hybrid regimes, especially in Francophone Africa in which the elections that are conducted are predetermined, though the stakeholders fake the whole process as democratic, thereby disguising the authoritarianism of their political systems under a thin veil of electoral legitimacy. The game plan also involves their puppet masters—the big powers, usually Western—giving their approval to the masquerade with messages of congratulation to the incumbents or their chosen successors, thereby effectively recognizing the results of the election, and sustaining the comprador and system in place against the interests of people and the country. Compaore was trying to emulate Paul Biya of Cameroon (in power since 1982), who changed the constitution of the country again in 2008 to allow him two seven-year terms in office, and then used his security forces to crush the Cameroonians who came out to the streets to show their disapproval, killing 150 protesters in the process, but he was not as astute as his Cameroonian counterpart who was even more unpopular but managed to pull off the gamble.

An autopsy report, which was conducted on the exhumed remains of Thomas Sankara, revealed that the anti-imperialist revolutionary died from dozens of gunshot wounds, ruling out the feeble claim that his assassins killed him by mistake, as his onetime closest friend and successor tried to convince the world after his death. As Ambroise Farama, one of the lawyers representing the Sankara family, said, it was *"...mind-boggling...You could say he was purely and simply riddled with bullets"*. On the contrary, the autopsies on the bodies of the other 12 soldiers killed and buried with Sankara in 1987 revealed that they had suffered only one or two gunshot wounds.

Burkina Faso restored Thomas Sankara's legacy as a revolutionary, a pan-Africanist, an environmentalist, a feminist, and a humanitarian with a bronze statue in the capital city of Ouagadougou in March 2019. However, the statue would be corrected a year later in May 2020, making it more imposing and truer to life than the previous one.

A statue of Thomas Sankara in May 2020

Three decades after the assassination of Thomas Sankara, the youths of Africa who are trying to find their bearings still reserve a high place for the African revolutionary icon as one of those rare contemporary figures that the continent has produced that can be hailed as a model and a figure to identify with. His legacy is rapidly expanding beyond Africa as more and more people recognize him as a precursor of environmental struggle, as an outstanding figure in the case against financial globalism, as an advocate for the non-payment of illegitimate debts, and as a prototype of self-reliant development against the liberal model of development that benefits only a small minority.

As a matter of fact, today, numerous books, articles and other works of art glorify the selfless African legend who took upon himself the colossal task of putting the people on their feet and showing them the path to a future devoid of neocolonialist influence that is wrapped up in trade, finance and imported cultures that undermine the strength of African communalist values and the sacredness of the family.

Democracy Index: Africa and the World

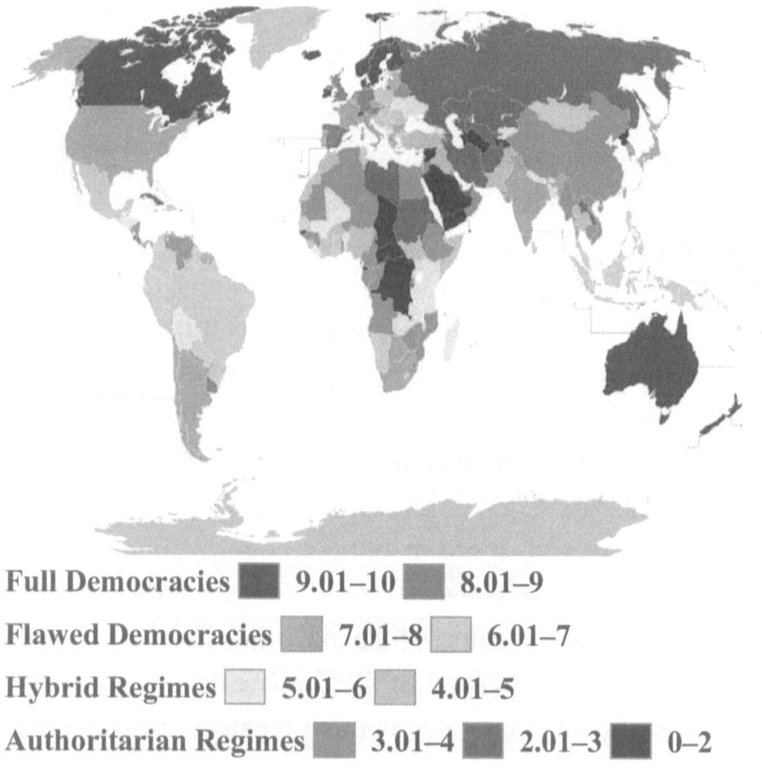

African Countries

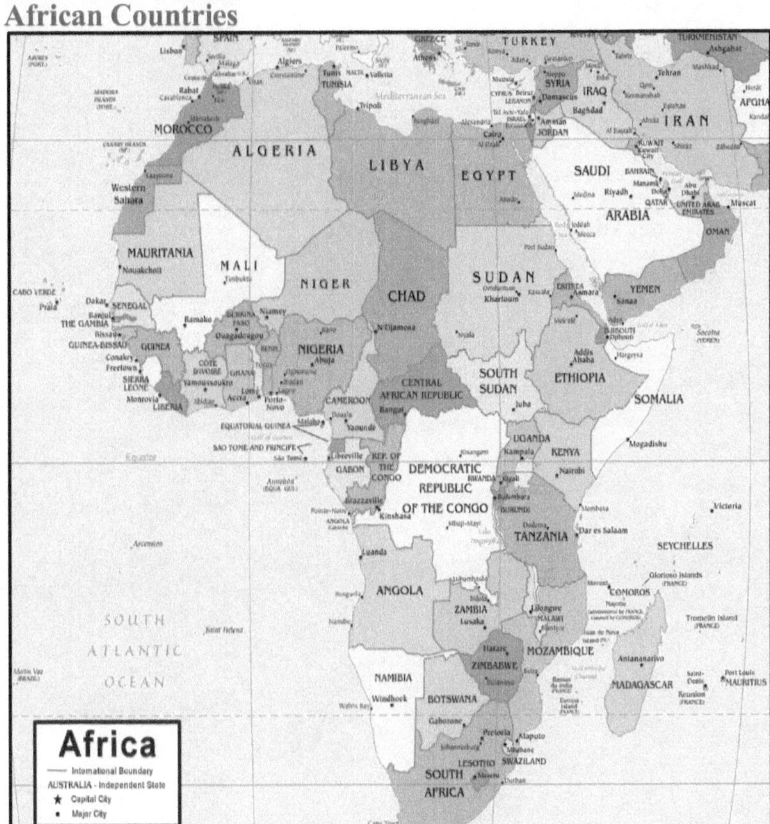

Chapter Four

Muammar al-Qaddafi

MUAMMAR QADDAFI QUOTES

"There must be a world revolution which puts an end to all materialistic conditions hindering woman from performing her natural role in life and driving her to carry out man's duties in order to be equal in rights."

"Nations whose nationalism is destroyed are subject to ruin."

"Man's freedom is lacking if somebody else controls what he needs, for need May result in man's enslavement of man."

"Once a ruler becomes religious, it becomes impossible for you to debate with him. Once someone rules in the name of religion, your lives become hell."

"Let the free people of the world know that we could have bargained over and sold out our cause in return for a personal, secure, and stable life. We received many offers to this effect, but we chose to be at the vanguard of the confrontation as a badge of duty and honor."

"I have nothing but scorn for the notion of an Islamic bomb. There is no such thing as an Islamic bomb or a Christian bomb. Any such weapon is a means of terrorizing humanity, and we are against the manufacture and acquisition of nuclear weapons. This is in line with our definition of and opposition to terrorism."

"I won't be a party to a conspiracy to mobilize the Arabs against the Persians. Only the forces of colonialism benefit from such a conspiracy. I won't be a party to a conspiracy that splits Islam into two - Shiite Islam and Sunni Islam - mobilizing Sunni Islam against Shiite Islam."

"The times of Arab nationalism and unity are gone forever. These ideas, which mobilized the masses, are only a worthless currency. Libya has had to put up with too much from the Arabs for whom it has poured forth both blood and money."

Maps

Libya on a map of the world

Libya and the Arab World

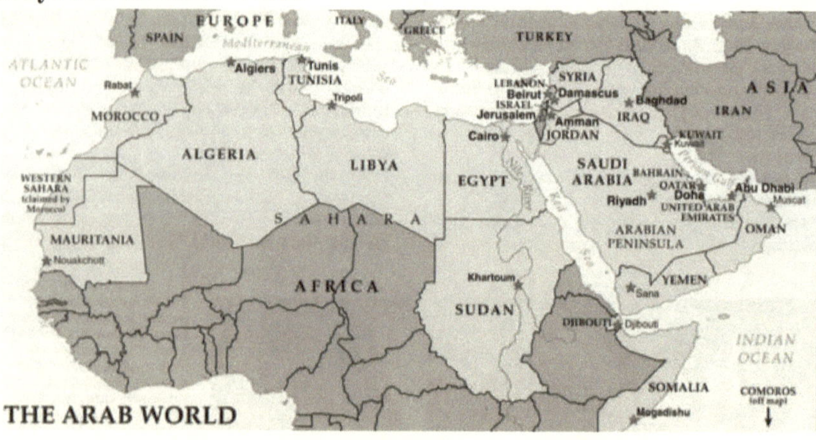

Libya on a map of Africa

The Arab Spring

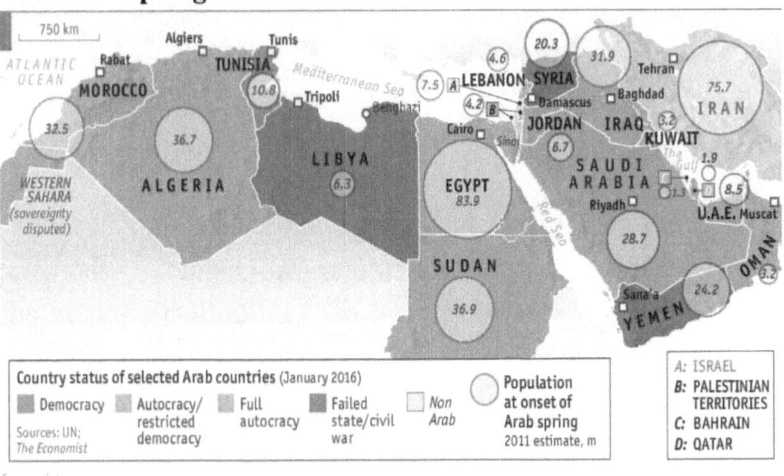

Country status of selected Arab countries (January 2016)

Democracy — Autocracy/restricted democracy — Full autocracy — Failed state/civil war — Non Arab

Population at onset of Arab spring 2011 estimate, m

A: ISRAEL
B: PALESTINIAN TERRITORIES
C: BAHRAIN
D: QATAR

Sources: UN; The Economist

Economist.com

For a little while longer, the story of Muammar al-Qaddafi shall continue to feature in major political discourses throughout Africa and the Middle East, and his life and especially death would, every now and then, be a source of satisfaction, irritation, controversy, rue, anger, and disgust in the rest of the world.

How did this divisive figure who dominated Libyan politics for four decades, who supported Arab and then African unity, who brought significant improvements to the quality of life of Libyans, making them the envy of the rest of Africa, and who was lauded by some for his anti-imperialist stance, end up isolated, haunted by NATO (North Atlantic Treaty Organization) and finally got killed by Libyans in a civil war where his foreign enemies fought with the Libyan rebels? Why was he strongly opposed by Islamic fundamentalists, condemned by Western powers as a dictator who violated the human rights of his people and financed global terrorism, and why was he kept at arm's length by those he wanted to work with?

We can find some of the answers in the account below.

The controversial Muammar al-Qaddafi, who was Africa's longest-serving head of state until his ouster and death on October 20, 2011, was born on June 7, 1942, to a tribal family called the al-Qadhafah in the central coastal settlement of Sirte, Libya, at a time that Libya was an Italian colony. Qaddafi barely knew what was going on around him when Libya gained independence in 1951 as the United Kingdom of Libya, and as a constitutional and hereditary monarchy under Western-allied King Idris. However, the Arab nationalist movement would greatly influence him as a young man, and he would admire its leader, the Egyptian strongman Gamal Abdel Nasser, to the point where he decided to become a soldier like his Egyptian hero, a dream he fulfilled by entering the military college in the eastern Libyan city of Benghazi in 1961. He would eventually spend four months of military training in the United Kingdom.

Partition Map of Africa

In Libya, Qaddafi steadily rose through the ranks of the military as the exploitation of oil brought wealth into the country. However, disaffection grew over the increased concentration of the nation's wealth in the hands of King

Idris. It was during this time that the talented and charismatic Qaddafi became involved with a movement of young officers bent on overthrowing the king. He would eventually rise to power in the group to the position of leadership. On September 1, 1969, the group overthrew King Idris while he was abroad in Turkey for medical treatment and named Qaddafi the commander-in-chief of the armed forces and chairman of the Revolutionary Command Council — Libya's new ruling body, effectively making him the ruler of Libya at the age of twenty-seven.

One of the early measures the new authorities took to stamp their authority over the North African country was the immediate shutting down of the American and British military bases in Libya and their forceful demand that foreign oil companies in the country share a bigger proportion of revenue with Libya. That same year, they forbade the sale of alcohol and replaced the Gregorian calendar with the Islamic one.

A failed coup attempt by his fellow officers in December 1969 would make Qaddafi put into place laws criminalizing political dissent. He would go on to expel the remaining Italians from Libya in 1970 and emphasized what he saw as a battle between Arab nationalism and Western imperialism. This would also see him vocally opposing Zionism and Israel, culminating in his expulsion of the Jewish community from the country. As relations with the West soured further and further, Qaddafi's inner circle of trusted people became smaller and smaller, resulting in a police state whose intelligence agents were audacious enough to even go after Libyans living in exile whom they deemed to be working with the enemies of the Libyan state.

The early years of Qaddafi's rule saw him making vigorous attempts to orient Libya away from the West and towards the Middle East and Africa. However, Libya would get into a military conflict with Egypt and Sudan after they tilted towards the West following the signing of the Egyptian-Israeli peace agreement between Nasser's successor, Anwar Sadat and the right-wing prime minister of Israel, Menachem Begin. Libya would even get involved in the bloody civil war in Chad against the pro-French faction in the conflict.

When, in the 1970s, Qaddafi published the first volume of the Green Book, which is a three-volume work describing the problems inherent in liberal democracy and capitalism, he raised eyebrows because his opponents saw it as more than an explanation of his political philosophy. In fact, the book was aimed at promoting his policies as the remedy for the outlined problems. His other claims that their New Libya boasted popular committees and shared ownership generated concerns in several quarters, even though the ideas in the book were not reflected on the ground in Libya, the way he claimed.

Even as the wellbeing of the average Libyan under his rule became better to the point of becoming the best in Africa, Qaddafi's foreign enemies were not the only ones who noticed a dose of eccentricity in his style of rule. The fact that he was having a cadre of female bodyguards in heels even though Libya was a Muslim country perched in a region where the issues of women's rights were still a social backwater; the fact that he considered himself the king of Africa after some African leaders appreciated his drive for an African Union and so awarded him the title; the fact that he was known to erect a tent to stay in when he traveled abroad; the fact that he dressed in outfits that though recognizable in several parts of Africa, did not fit the diplomatic norm; the fact that he was not politically correct and often spoke his mind in a world where most leaders preferred to keep things under the radar; and the fact he would not let Libya become the vassal of any of the big powers, made him a loose cannon in many of the circles of power.

From Left to Right: Muammar Qaddafi, Yasser Arafat of the Palestinian Liberation Organization, Egypt's Abdel Nasser, and King Hussein of Jordan (1970)

Ronald Reagan, the 40th president of the United States of America would call Qaddafi "The Mad Dog of the Middle East" after concluding that the Libyan leader was not only ruthless in clamping down on dissent against his autocratic rule at home while his agents hunted down and killed opponents abroad, but also that his government was implicated in the financing of many anti-Western groups around the world, including groups considered to be terrorist organizations like the Baader Meinhof of Germany, The Japanese Red Brigade, The Irish Republican Party and the numerous Palestinian groups fighting against Israel. The fact that he was also supporting several liberation movements in Africa such as the African National Congress (ANC) in its campaign against Apartheid South Africa, the MPLA (*Movimento Popular de Libertação de Angola*)—"People's Movement for the Liberation of Angola"—against the Portuguese colonial master in Angola, the FRELIMO (*Frente de Libertação de Moçambique*)—"Liberation Front of Mozambique"— against Portuguese colonial rule in Mozambique, SWAPO (South West Africa People's Organization) against South African colonial rule in Namibia, and the Polisario Front or simply POLISARIO (*Frente Popular de Liberación de Saguía el Hamra y Río de Oro*) — "Popular Front for the Liberation of Saguia el-Hamra and Río de Oro" — against the Moroccan occupation of the former Spanish Western Sahara in defiance of the collective wish of the people of the territory and the international community; and the fact that he financed coups against African heads of state he considered Western puppets, made him an irritant in the world of "civilized nations".

Following a 1986 bombing of a West Berlin dance club in Germany that killed three and injured scores of people, the United States of America blamed Libya for the terror attack and the US. President Ronald Reagan ordered the bombing of specific targets in Libya, including Qaddafi's residence in the Libyan capital city of Tripoli. In the campaign, the United States lost an aircraft that was shot down, resulting in the deaths of two of its crew members. Qaddafi was not killed in the military campaign, but Libya lost 45 soldiers and officials and 15–30 civilians, including a young girl Qaddafi claimed was her adopted daughter, called Hanna. In addition, dozens of the North African country's military hardware were destroyed.

Libya was accused of carrying out the 1988 Lockerbie bombing when a plane carrying 259 people blew up near Lockerbie, Scotland, killing all of the passengers on board. The resulting falling debris would kill an additional 11 civilians on the ground. The United Nations put Libya under sanctions on the grounds that it was implicated in the bombing. But that was not all about it. Several Libyans, including a Qaddafi in-law, were also believed to be behind the explosion of the French passenger jet UTA Flight 772 in 1989, killing all 170 passengers on board the aircraft, including Bonnie Barnes Pugh, the wife of Robert L. Pugh, the United States ambassador to the Republic of Chad, which is Libya's principal southern neighbor.

There is a school of thought that the rapprochement that began in the 1990s between Libya and the West came about because of Qaddafi's West-leaning sons, who managed to convince the Libyan leader that all would be fine if he mended ties with the Western powers. However, the thawing of the relationship between Qaddafi and the West was happening at a time of growing threat from Islamists who opposed his rule. He started sharing information with the British and American intelligence services on containing and neutralizing this growing Islamic fundamentalism.

Qaddafi and the South African and World Icon Nelson Mandela

So, when in 1994, the new president of South Africa and head of the country's ruling party (African National Congress — ANC) Nelson Mandela (he had spent 27 years in Apartheid jail before his release in 1990 that began the peaceful process in the dismantling of Apartheid) visited Libya even though the North African country was under an international travel ban, the Western powers were not happy about it. However, Nelson Mandela persuaded the Libyan leader to hand over the two Libyan nationals whom the United States of America and its Western allies suspected of plotting the Lockerbie bombing. The world was surprised that Qaddafi agreed to do so. The Libyan leader trusted

Nelson Mandela, who turned out to be the only foreign leader to visit Libya during the two-decade embargo on the country and a decade of flight ban. The former South African political prisoner and president at the time made the demanding land journey from Egypt to Libya in appreciation of Libya's fervent support for the South African anti-Apartheid forces in their struggle against the white minority rule of the Apartheid system in South Africa. The anti-Apartheid icon and renowned South African statesman's visit marked the beginning of the mending of relations with the West on many fronts and appeared to many to herald a new era in Libyan-Western relations. In fact, it was during the 1990s that Qaddafi stopped giving financial, material, and human support to the various Pan-Arab and Pan-African movements, especially the Palestinian groups. Instead, he focused on getting sanctions on Libya lifted. Some say he gave up on the Palestinians after Yasser Arafat's Palestinian Liberation Organization (PLO) failed to inform him of the secret negotiations they were conducting with the Israelis that eventually led to the signing of the September 13, 1993, Oslo I Accords on reaching a peace deal between Israel and the Palestinians. His pariah status at the time came about mostly from Libya's actions in support of the Palestinians.

The September 11, 2001, terrorist attacks in the United States of America would alter the geostrategic landscape of the world, especially when George W. Bush, the 43rd president of the United States of America, stated that "Either you are with us, or you are against us." It was whispered in high circles shortly after those attacks that the United States intended to bring down the regimes in the countries George

Bush accused of being the "Axis of Evil", comprising Iran, Iraq, North Korea, Cuba, Libya, Sudan, and Syria. So, when Libya peacefully resolved with the United States of America in December 2003 to eliminate its weapons of mass destruction program, including a decades-old nuclear weapons program, many people doubted the Libyan leader's claim that his reason for wanting the program scrapped was that he did not want terrorists to get hold of those weapons. They held instead that Qaddafi got rid of his program of weapons of mass destruction because of threats made by the United States of America that he could not withstand, and so succumbed to American demands just to appease them.

Map of African Countries and the capitals

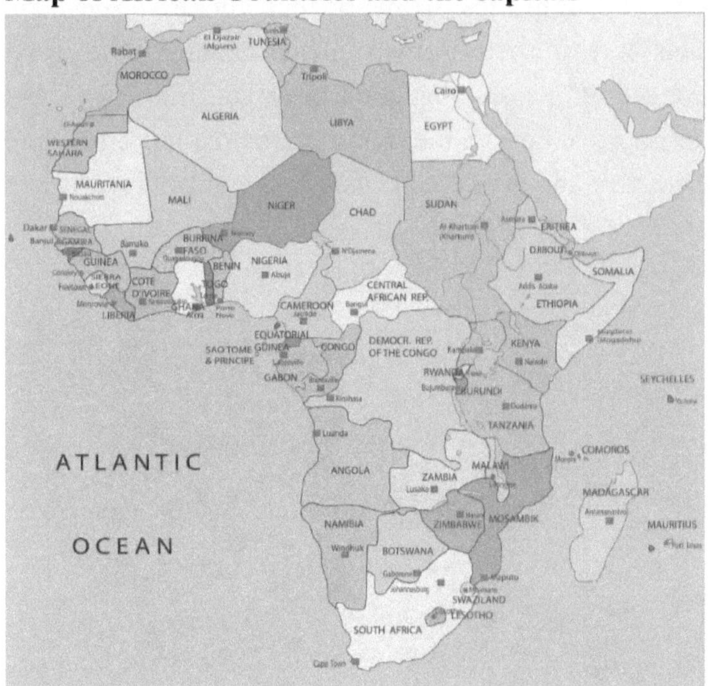

Many Qaddafi critics were not happy that the Libyan leader was welcomed in Western capitals. When the Italian Prime Minister Silvio Berlusconi boasted publicly that he was among Qaddafi's close friends, many critics of the Libyan strongman wondered whether the newfound friendship of Qaddafi and the West wasn't based on business and access to Libyan oil.

For years, Qaddafi's sons, and more especially his son and heir apparent, Seif al-Islam Qaddafi, mixed freely with London's high society and other high societies in several parts of Europe and America. As if to reward Libya and its strongman for "changing their ways", the United Nations eased sanctions on Libya in 2001, which made it easy for foreign oil companies to work out lucrative new oil contracts and to operate freely in the country. The result was not only a massive injection of capital into Libya, but also an improvement in the living standards, more freedom in the country and greater exposure to the outside world.

2010: Qaddafi and Other African Heads of State

When some Arabs accused Qaddafi of giving Israel a stronger strategic edge in the region with the disarmament, of giving credence to the United States doctrine of preemptive war, and of failing to get security guarantees for Libya and the Arab world, the Libyan government and its supporters responded that giving up its nuclear weapons program enabled Libya to return to the fold of the international community of nations, get a temporary United Nations Security Council seat, and save some money for investing in the Libyan people and in developing the country.

Many Qaddafi supporters, especially in Africa, hold that Qaddafi tapped Libya's economic resurgence into political capital in the continent and started promoting the quick realization of an African Economic Union with a gold-backed currency called the Dinar that would have effectively curtailed France's domineering neocolonialist role in Francophone Africa, thereby making him intolerable in the eyes of France and its Western allies. However, his critics think his dictatorial rule, obstinacy, and inability to adjust to the clamor for democracy and freedom sparked off the protest against his rule, a demand for a fundamental change of the system that degenerated into an uprising, and then into a civil war.

Qaddafi initially thought the Arab Spring that began in Libya's eastern neighbor Tunisia in January 2011 and then spread to its western neighbor Egypt the next month, resulting in the ouster of Zine El Abidine Ben Ali and Hosni Mubarak of Tunisia and Egypt, respectively, would bypass Libya. But that was not the case.

Qaddafi and French President Nicolas Sarkozy in 2007

He had been in power for four decades and could not be immune to the opposition. The political changes in Libya's eastern and western neighbors boosted the morale of citizens of the various Arab countries to protest. In Libya, demonstrations broke out in the eastern city of Benghazi, which is Libya's second-largest city and is known for its history of opposition to the capital city, Tripoli. The unrest then spread throughout Libya, despite the carrot and stick measures undertaken by the Qaddafi regime to abate the situation.

Qaddafi's early indecisive measures emboldened the protesters, and the standoff quickly degenerated into an armed uprising. His critics accused him of escalating the situation, of carrying out a bloody repression and of using foreign mercenaries. Qaddafi, on his part, claimed the demonstrators were traitors, foreigners, al-Qaeda followers, and drug addicts. He urged his supporters to continue the fight against the new resistance.

The rebels had formed a governing body called the National Transitional Council by the end of February 2011. At the end of March, a French-led NATO coalition began to provide support for the rebel forces in the form of airstrikes and a no-fly zone, with logistical support provided by the USA. NATO's military intervention over the next six months would destroy the Libyan Air Force and decimate the country's Armed Forces, so that most of those fighting for Qaddafi ended up being people who had no connection with the regular army. NATO's attacks proved to be decisive as one Libyan city after another fell into rebel hands and as an airstrike killed Qaddafi's youngest son, Saif al-Arab Qaddafi and three of Qaddafi's grandchildren while the Libyan leader and his wife, Safiyah (Safia), were attending a gathering of family and friends hosted by their son, Said al-Arab.

When, in June 2011, the International Criminal Court issued warrants for the arrest of Qaddafi, his son Seif al-Islam, and his brother-in-law for crimes against humanity, the world understood that the powers that be had completely disavowed Qaddafi and that there was no future for his regime. When a month after the indictments, more than 30 countries recognized the NTC as the legitimate government of Libya, it was understood that Qaddafi had lost the civil war.

Tripoli, the capital, fell to rebel forces in late August 2011, bringing about a symbolic end to Qaddafi's rule as he retreated to Sirte, his hometown, even though most of his enemies could not say for certain where he was. He had basically lost control of Libya, but his whereabouts could not be ascertained.

So, when on October 20, 2011, the world learned that Muammar al-Qaddafi had died near his hometown of Sirte, Libya, after a NATO aerial attack on his convoy forced him to hide in a ditch, whence he was discovered by enemy fighters who proceeded to kill him, many people found the news disquieting. However, videos surfaced, showing Qaddafi's bloodied body being dragged around by rebel fighters, then his dead body on display, the last live moments of his other son, Mutassim Qaddafi, and later of Mutassim's lifeless body after he had been executed. While news of Qaddafi's death spread around, spurring many Libyans to pour into the streets in celebration of what many of them hailed as the culmination of their revolution and the start of a new chapter in their history, others saw it as proof that former colonial powers who did not have the interests of the Libyan people at heart, had succeeded in defeating a major bulwark against further or continuous foreign exploitation and control of Libya and Africa. This sentiment was deeply felt in the Middle East, and more especially in Africa, where news had reached many people in the countries there that Qaddafi had stashed away gold and silver valued at more than $7 billion, which he intended for use to establish a pan-African currency based on the Libyan golden Dinar, a currency that would have provided the countries of Francophone African with an alternative currency to the French Franc (CFA) that is considered in many circles as one of the tools of French exploitation and strangulation of its former colonies and territories in Africa.

Tribal and Ethnic Map of Libya

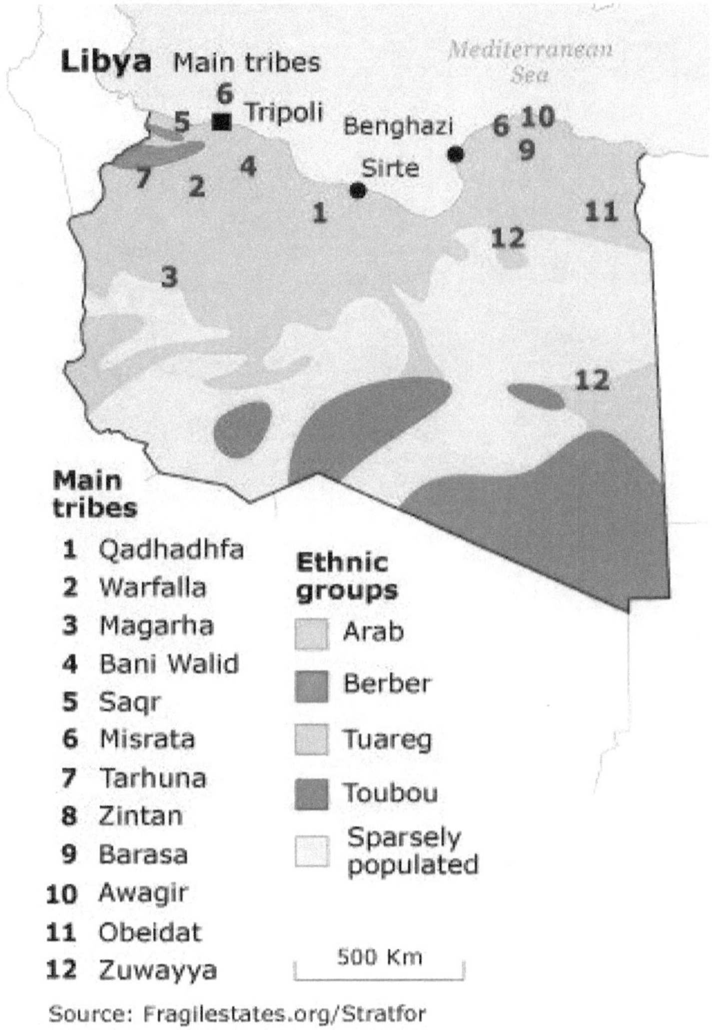

Source: Fragilestates.org/Stratfor

Post-Qaddafi Factional Division of Libya 2016

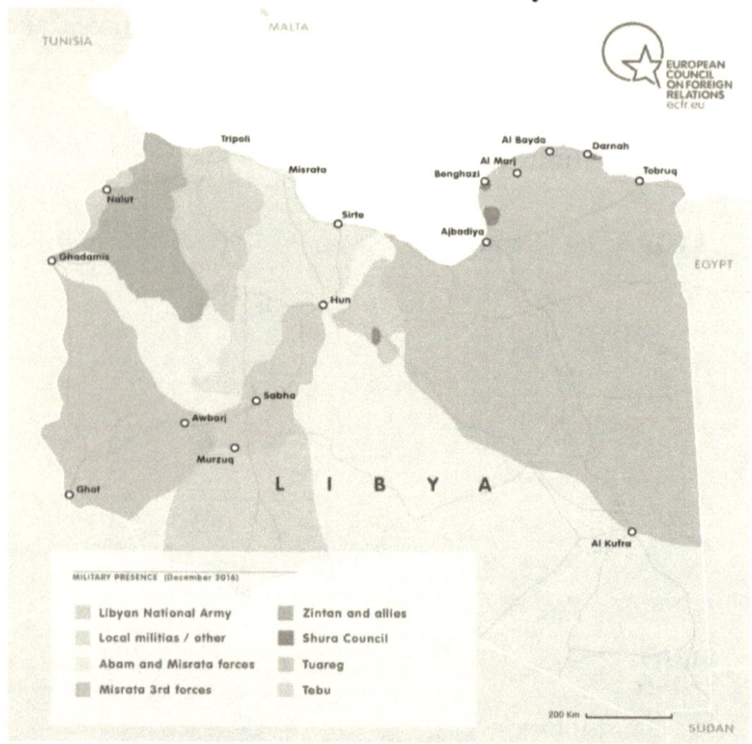

Today

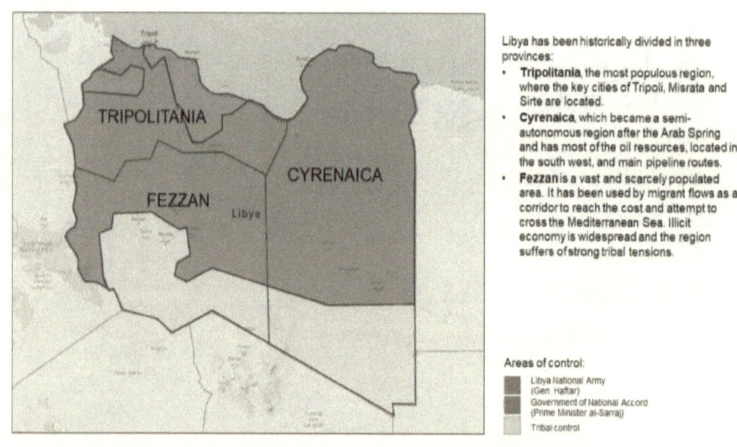

Libya has been historically divided in three provinces:

- **Tripolitania**, the most populous region, where the key cities of Tripoli, Misrata and Sirte are located.
- **Cyrenaica**, which became a semi-autonomous region after the Arab Spring and has most of the oil resources, located in the south west, and main pipeline routes.
- **Fezzan** is a vast and scarcely populated area. It has been used by migrant flows as a corridor to reach the cost and attempt to cross the Mediterranean Sea. Illicit economy is widespread and the region suffers of strong tribal tensions.

Areas of control:

The media, especially in the Middle East, speculated that the overthrow and killing of Qaddafi would make Iran, North Korea, and possibly other countries more reluctant to give up their nuclear programs and/or nuclear weapons due to the risk of being weakened and/or double-crossed afterwards. Many people in Africa accused the big powers of double-standards, wondering why the Western powers have been rubbing shoulders with African dictators like Paul Biya of Cameroon (in power since 1982), the Bongos (Omar, from December 02, 1967 – June 08, 2009, and now his son Ali since October 16 2009), the Eyademas (Gnassingbé, from April 14, 1967 – February 5, 2005, and his son Faure Essozimna since May 04, 2005), dictators who impoverished their people, are loathed across the board, and who flagrantly rig elections to stay in power — a sacrilege to democracy that their puppeteers turn a blind eye to or give their blessings to.

As post-Qaddafi Libya continues to be embroiled in violence eight years after his death, as armed Islamists make the country ungovernable, as warlords and armed militias abound and create a situation that makes Libya a collection of fiefdoms, as two rival governments reign in the country, many wonder whether Libya would be able to come up any time soon with a functioning system that is better than the rule of the heavily flawed, power-hungry, ruthless but patriotic Muammar Qaddafi who failed to leave behind a peaceful legacy that could be emulated by future generations, a failure that is making it possible for the foreign forces he had ardently wished to keep out of Libya to have a free hand in shaping or in failing to shape the country's future.

The ripple effect of the Libyan civil-war spread across North and West Africa, as thousands of combatants, mostly ethnic Tuaregs from Mali and Niger who supported either Qaddafi or the NTC during the conflict, returned to their home countries with a wide range of weapons and ammunition, setting off a trail of civil conflicts in Niger, Mali, Algeria, Nigeria, Cameroon, Chad, and the Central African Republic. Today, there is little clamor for an African Economic Union as no other African head of state has stepped forward to lead the effort after the death of Qaddafi, leaving the continent today as the last frontier in a new quest by the industrial powers of the world to secure rapidly dwindling resources.

Democracy Index: Africa and the World

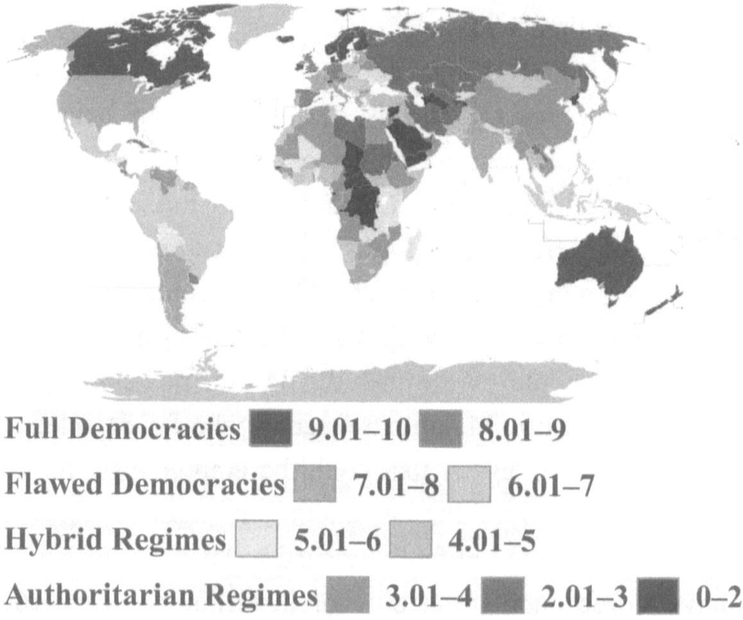

African Countries

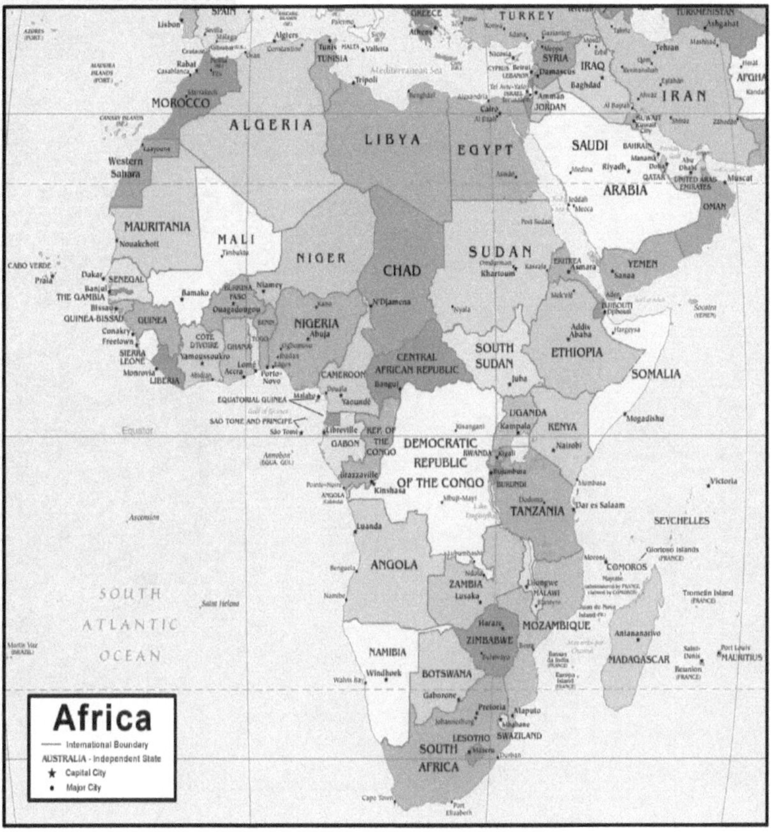

Chapter Five

Anwar al-Sadat

Anwar al-Sadat Quotes

"Peace is much more precious than a piece of land... let there be no more wars."

"He who cannot change the very fabric of his thought will never be able to change reality."

"There can be hope only for a society which acts as one big family, not as many separate ones."

"Most people seek after what they do not possess and are enslaved by the very things they want to acquire."

"Fear is, I believe, a most effective tool in destroying the soul of an individual - and the soul of a people."

"Great suffering has a silver lining that we can be grateful for, because it builds up a human being and puts him or her within reach of self-knowledge."

"This [fundamentalism] is not religion. It is an obscenity. These are lies, the criminal use of religious power to misguide people."

"There is no happiness for people at the expense of other people."

"I believe that for peace, a man may, even should, do everything in his power. Nothing in this world could rank higher than peace."

"If you don't have the capacity to change yourself and your own attitudes, then nothing around you can be changed."

"Russians can give you arms, but only the United States can give you a solution."

"I do not care for socially recognizable success. I only value that success which I can feel within me, which satisfies me, and which basically stems from self-knowledge."

"To love means to give, and to give means to build, while to hate is to destroy."

"I was brought up to believe that how I saw myself was more important than how others saw me."

"Let there be no more war or bloodshed between Arabs and Israelis. Let there be no more suffering or denial of rights. Let there be no more despair or loss of faith."

"Real success is success with self. It's not in having things, but in having mastery, having victory over self."

"Faith means that a man should regard any disaster simply as a fate-determined blow which must be endured."

"Only when he has ceased to need things can a man truly be his own master and so really exist."

"Land is immortal, for it harbors the mysteries of creation."

"Let every girl, let every woman, let every mother here [in Israel] — and there in my country [Egypt] — know we shall solve all our problems through negotiations around the table rather than starting a war."

MAPS

Egypt on a map of the world

Partition Map of Africa

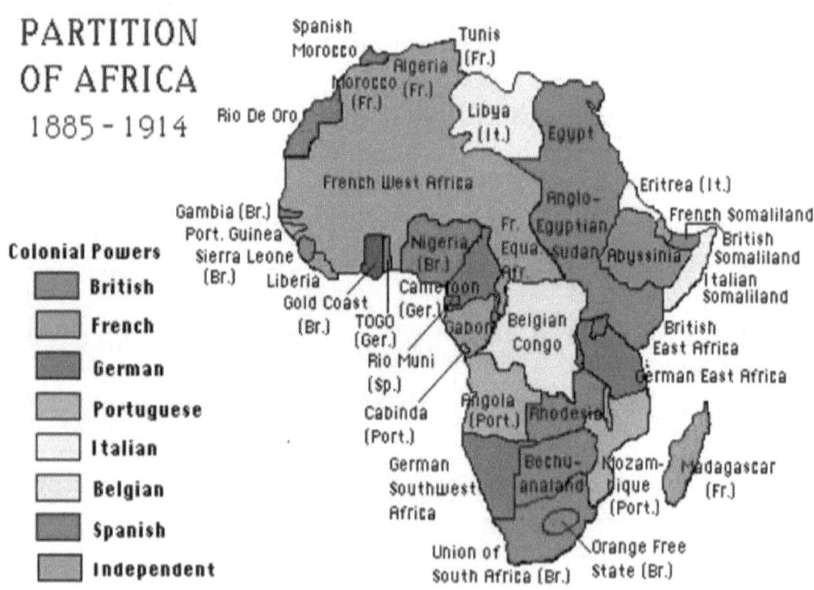

Map of African Countries and the capitals

Evaluations on the Democracy of African Countries

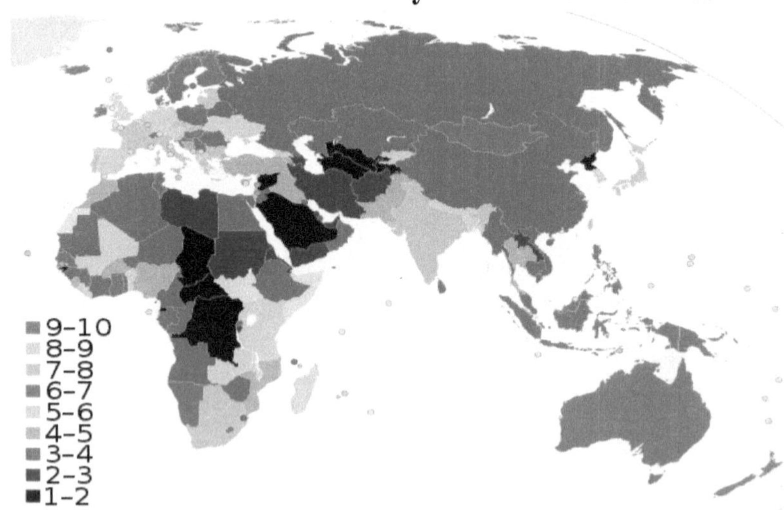

The Measure of Freedom of Countries of the World

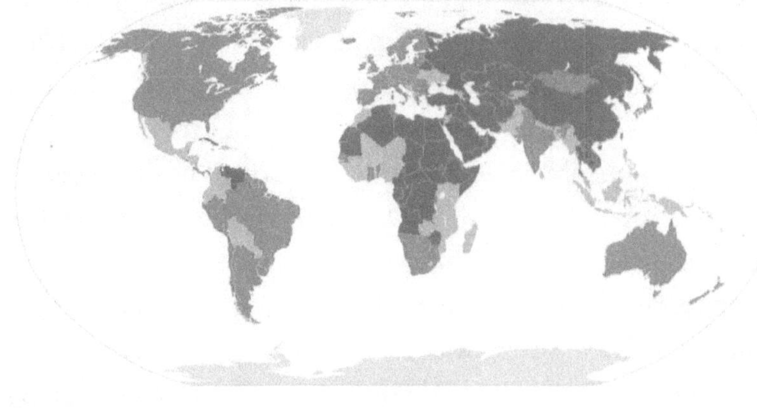

Anwar al-Sadat was born in Upper Egypt on December 25, 1918, into a family of 13 children, and grew up 40 miles north of Cairo at a time that Egypt was a British protectorate. The status of Egypt under the control of the British Empire came about from the crippling debt that forced the Egyptian government to sell its interests in the French-engineered Suez Canal to the British government.

Constructed between 1859 and 1869, the Suez Canal is an artificial sea-level waterway in Egypt that connects the Mediterranean Sea to the Red Sea through the Isthmus of Suez. The canal offers watercraft a shorter journey between the North Atlantic and the northern Indian Ocean, thereby reducing the journey by approximately 7,000 kilometers (4,300 miles). In fact, the British and the French had been using the resources of the canal to establish enough political control over Egypt that it was logical to refer to Egypt as a British colony.

Sadat would be greatly affected by four figures in his early life:

- Zahran from Sadat's home village, who was hanged by the British for a riot that resulted in the death of a British officer
- Kemal Ataturk, who created the modern state of Turkey from the ashes of the Ottoman Empire
- Mohandas (Mahatma) Gandhi, who had preached the power of nonviolence in combating injustice while touring Egypt in 1932
- And finally, Adolf Hitler, who was initially regarded by Sadat as someone who could help unshackle Egypt from British colonial control.

When the British created a military school in Egypt in 1936, following an agreement with the Egyptian Wafd party, Sadat became one of its first students. After his graduation, the government posted him to Sudan, where he met Gamal Abdel Nasser, with whom, along with several other junior officers, he formed the secret Free Officers, a movement dedicated to the revolution that would free Egypt and Sudan from the domination of the British and the corruption of the monarchy. This political association would eventually lead them to the Egyptian presidency.

Sadat would be jailed twice for his revolutionary activities during the Second World War. This was precisely for his efforts to obtain help from the Axis Powers (Italy and Germany) to expel the British. After his release from prison, he reconnected with Nasser only to find out that their movement had grown considerably during the years that he was incarcerated. On July 23, 1952, the Free Officers Organization overthrew King Farouk and brought an end to the Egyptian monarchy in a military coup d'état that launched the Egyptian Revolution of 1952. Thereafter, he became Nasser's public relations minister and trusted lieutenant. The hardworking and focused Sadat would accomplish Nasser's order to oversee the official abdication of King Farouk.

It was during Nasser's years in power that Sadat learned the dangerous game of nation-building in a world of superpower rivalries. They led Egypt into becoming a "non-aligned" state, hence making the North African country one of the leading nations that underdeveloped and post-colonial societies looked up to. Nasser and Sadat would survive the 1956 war after Nasser nationalized the Suez Canal, prompting the British, the French, and the Israelis to launch an attack on Egypt in a bid to wrest control of the canal from Egyptian hands. The 1956 war would only end after the United States of America forced Britain, France, and Israel to withdraw their forces from Egypt. The two comrades exploited that war to the point where Egypt emerged from that conflict as a champion of the non-aligned countries for resisting the big powers.

Nasser's prominence would take a beating from the debacle of the 1967 Six-Day War when the Israeli military destroyed the Egyptian air forces and incapacitated the Egyptian Army by killing at least 3,000 soldiers and occupying the Sinai Peninsula all the way to the Suez Canal. The outcome of the war put a strain on the Egyptian economy and almost bankrupted the government. What was even more disheartening for Nasser was the growing disunity among the squabbling Arab nations and the growing Palestinian movements. His death on September 29, 1970, from a heart attack, came about from his declining health caused by Egypt's defeat in the 1967 Arab-Israeli war.

Called "Nasser's black poodle" by some Egyptians of high ranking, Sadat was underrated when he succeeded Nasser. However, he proved himself over the next 11 years to be an astute leader of his people. When he openly offered the Israelis a peace treaty in exchange for the Sinai Peninsula captured by Israel in the 1967 war, many, especially in the Arab world, were taken aback. Still, he would surmount the domestic crisis and international intrigues that plagued his presidency. He would make the Soviet Union take him seriously by expelling them after they failed to replenish Egypt's depleted military supplies, and then he would repair relations with them again.

Map of Israel and its neighbors following the 1967 War

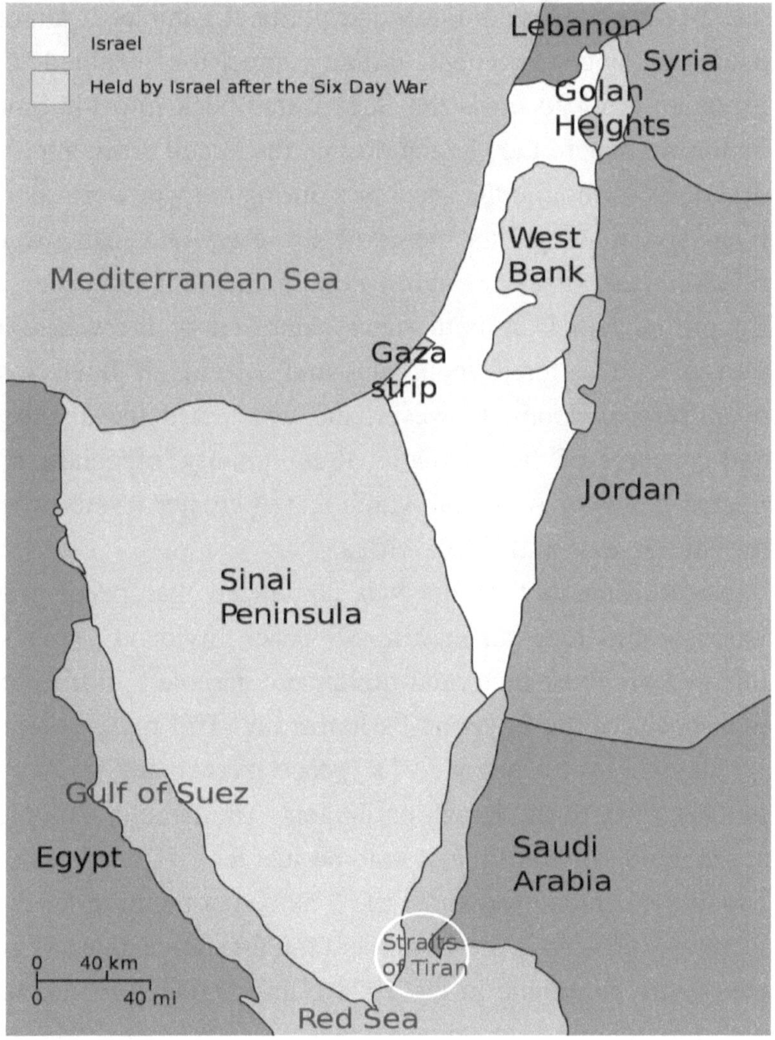

When, on October 6, 1973, Sadat ordered the Egyptian Army to attack Israel in coordination with the Syrian Army under the country's strongman Hafez al-Assad, it was in a bid to recapture the Sinai Peninsula following the Jewish state's continuous refusal of Egypt's peace initiative. Dubbed the Yom Kippur War but also known as the Ramadan War, it was Sadat's biggest military and political gamble. It almost paid off since excellent military precision enabled the Egyptian army to cross the Suez Canal back into the Sinai Peninsula, where they began driving the Israeli army into the desert. Even though the successes during the war were short-lived and much of the gains of the Egyptian Army were reversed, the attack created a new momentum for peace in Egypt and Israel, as both states came out of the war war-weary, with battered economies and a sense of how close they were to doom. However, the war raised the attention and concerns of the international community, especially the United States of America, which feared greater instability in the Middle East and North Africa.

Sadat came out of the war convinced that peace with Israel would reap an enormous "peace dividend", and so initiated his most important diplomatic gamble by affirming in a speech to the Egyptian Parliament in 1977 that he would go anywhere to negotiate a peace agreement with the Israelis, even to the Israeli parliament. The Israelis took him at his word with an invitation to do just that — address the Israeli parliament known as the Knesset, something he did, thereby initiating a new momentum for peace that would eventually culminate in the 1978 Camp David Accords and with Egypt and Israel signing a final peace treaty in 1979. He and the Israeli Prime Minister Menachem Begin would win the Nobel Prize for Peace that year for their efforts in realizing peace between their two states.

The March 26, 1979, signing of the historic peace treaty between Israel and Egypt at the White House in Washington, DC. From left to right: Anwar Sadat, Jimmy Carter, Menachem Begin

Even though the peace treaty with Israel made it possible for Egypt to get the Sinai back and even though the country gets assistance from the West in the form of foreign aid, especially from the United States of America, assistance that has been helping the Egyptian economy recover and even prosper, it left Egypt shunned by the rest of the Arab world. Sadat's coziness with the West and the peace treaty with Israel also stirred up a great deal of domestic opposition, especially among the country's fundamentalist

Muslim groups. Even though he improved the everyday life of the common Egyptian, even though he made Sharia the basis of all new Egyptian laws, and even though he sought to restore calm to the nation by enacting laws outlawing protest, Muslim fundamentalists would not be satisfied.

It was that dissatisfaction that led to the assassination of Sadat on October 6, 1981, during a military parade celebrating the successful Suez crossing by the Egyptian Army during the 1973 War against Israel. His Vice President, Hosni Mubarak, would succeed him.

Three US. Presidents — Gerald Ford, Jimmy Carter, and Richard Nixon would attend Sadat's funeral. The only Arab head of state to pay his last honor to the assassinated Egyptian leader was Gaafar Nimeiry of Sudan, a move that would cost him dearly because Islamists overthrew him on April 6, 1985.

Even though Sadat's bold step in making peace with Israel cost him his life and led to Egypt's expulsion from the Arab League, it opened the door for future negotiations between Israel and the rest of the Arab world, making it possible for the Oslo Accords between Israel and the Palestinian Liberation Organization (PLO), which was signed in 1993. The signing of the peace treaty between Israel and Jordan in 1994, making Jordan the second Arab country to conclude peace with Israel, owes a lot to the pioneering peace that Sadat led Egypt to sign with Israel. Today, Israel has developed non-diplomatic ties with several other Arab countries and is recognized by several Muslim countries.

Sadat is honored in Malaysia, where he is an Honorary

"Grand Commander of the Order of the Defender of the Realm".

Today, close to four decades after the death of Anwar Sadat, if you ask Egyptians who knew him, experienced his rule or learned about his life story their opinion of his life and death, you are likely to get mixed reactions as answers to some of the views held about a fascinating man who led a complex country during a complicated period in the history of the most problematic region of the world. However, the emotions you will see on their faces the most would be those reflecting respect, gratitude, and pain.

Most secular Egyptians embrace his legacy, holding that he was a daring leader, a visionary, a realist, a pragmatist, a humane person, and a genuine patriot unencumbered by idealism.

However, most of those who opposed Sadat and think that the assassinated Egyptian leader left behind a negative legacy, believe that he betrayed the Arab cause by making a separate peace with Israel, since, in their view, the Egyptian-Israeli peace accord is a change in the geopolitical configuration in the region that only promises more violence in the future. These opponents also think that the prosperity he promised would follow the signing of the Egyptian-Israeli peace treaty at Camp David in the USA was overhyped.

As a matter of fact, there are other Egyptians who go as far as attacking the fundamentals of his character, claiming that he was frequently deceitful, vain, and indolent, and that he even played the buffoon every now and then, especially to his superiors.

While most pundits agree that Sadat's predecessor Gamal Abdul Nasser put the bricks together for the foundation of the modern Egyptian state, another popular view is that Sadat completed the foundation of modern Egypt and shaped the country's internal and external development — socio-economic and political in a very fundamental way, setting Egypt on a trajectory that hardly any other Egyptian leader or political movement can sway it away from. And he did so at a time that most Arab regimes had fallen into "moral and political degeneracy", thereby freeing Egypt from their bankrupt policies.

The Consequences of the Six-Day War of 1967

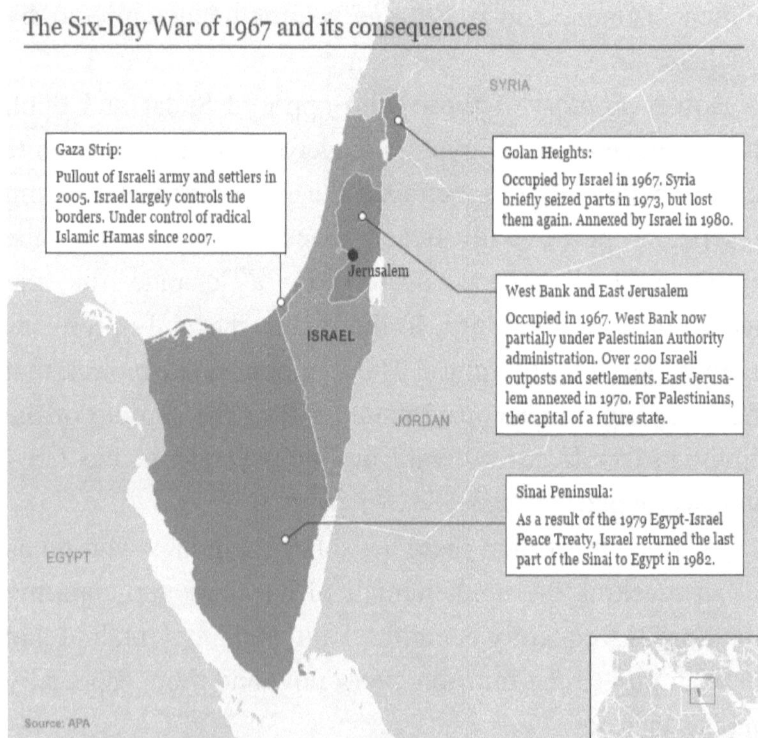

Sadat's critics, especially the harshest ones like the Islamists (The Muslim Brotherhood in particular), contend that he was repressive and hold him responsible for making it difficult for democracy to take root and grow in Egypt. Some of them even consider him an incompetent administrator who made a mockery of the law by repressing his real or imagined opponents, and who fostered corruption among his inner and outer circles.

No matter the position that a critique of Anwar Sadat takes, one thing that cannot be disputed is the fact that he inherited an Egypt from Gamal Abdul Nasser that was partially occupied by Israel, defeated, bankrupt, and heavily reliant on the Soviet Union, and he left it as a country that is more vibrant and secure.

Some pundits hold that Anwar Sadat was a visionary who understood that peace with Israel was inevitable, that the rest of the Arab World and the rest of the Muslim World would come around one day and make peace with Israel, and that the quicker it is done, the better. He could not convince his Arab and Muslim counterparts at the time to join him in his peace overtures and so went alone and concluded a peace treaty with Israel that brought Egypt dividends all right, but that earned it the resentment of the Arab and Muslim worlds.

Today, Anwar Sadat stands vindicated. Israel has grown stronger militarily, economically, and socially. Its population has almost quadrupled, and it is more entrenched in the occupied West Bank and Golan Heights than before. On the contrary, the positions of the Arab and

Muslim worlds vis-à-vis making peace with Israel have evolved to the point where the prevalent view is that they have mellowed tremendously. The destruction of Israel is no longer a mainstream position, and previously taboo topics are now subjects of negotiation. However, as it stands out, the realities on the ground in Israel and the occupied territories of the Golan Heights, the Gaza Strip, and the West Bank are changing every day in favor of those Israelis who are against a deal that involves the trading of land captured in the 1967 war for peace with the neighboring Arab peoples or countries. These are mostly right-wing Israelis who were a minority back in the 1970s, but whose numbers have been increasing every day as if mirroring the rise in Islamism and the radical parties among the Palestinian population that have embraced terrorism in their fight and commitment to make the land between the Jordan River and the mediterranean Sea Jew-free in a cause that is championed by the Islamic Resistance Movement, abbreviated Hamas, which, in June 2007, seized power from the Palestinian Authority in the Gaza Strip (that Israel disengaged from in 2005) and has been controlling this Palestinian territory since then.

Democracy Index: Africa and the World

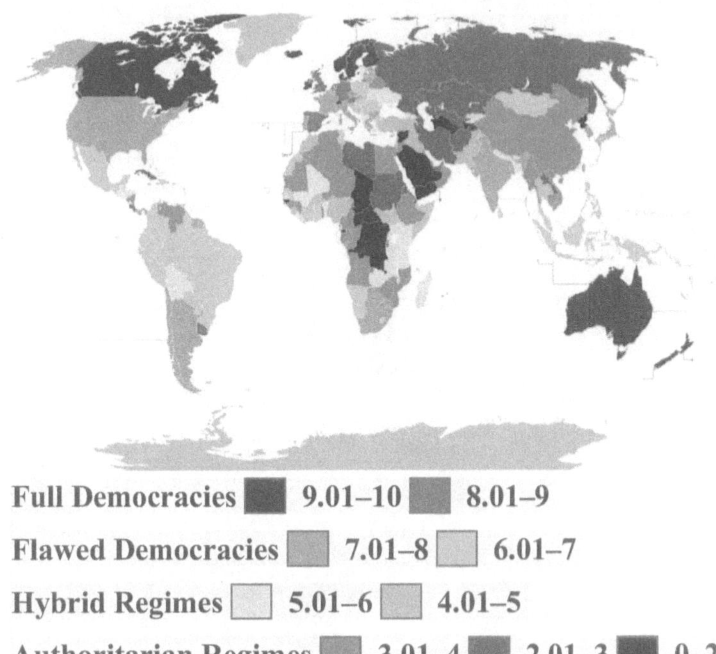

Full Democracies ▮ 9.01–10 ▮ 8.01–9

Flawed Democracies ▮ 7.01–8 ▮ 6.01–7

Hybrid Regimes ▮ 5.01–6 ▮ 4.01–5

Authoritarian Regimes ▮ 3.01–4 ▮ 2.01–3 ▮ 0–2

The Measure of Freedom of Countries of the World

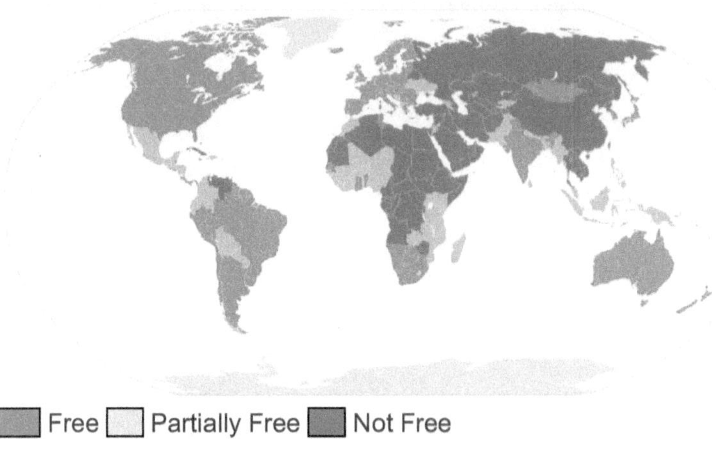

▮ Free ▮ Partially Free ▮ Not Free

African Countries

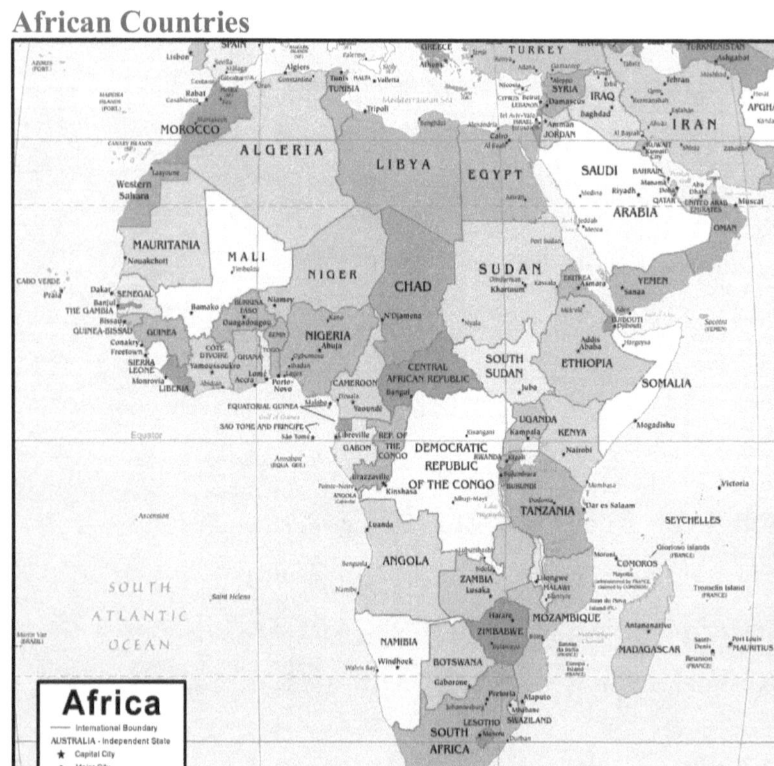

9 781980 996699